D0931725

INSIDE
AMERICA'S
CHRISTIAN
SCHOOLS

INSIDE
AMERICA'S
CHRISTIAN
SCHOOLS

B

BY
PAUL F. PARSONS

MERCER UNIVERSITY PRESS

Lennessee Tech. Library
Cookeville. Tenn.

380247

ISBN 0-86554-294-5   MUP/H258

Inside America's Christian Schools
Copyright ©1987
Mercer University Press, Macon, Georgia 31207
All rights reserved
Printed in the United States of America

The paper used in this publication meets
the minimum requirements of American National Standard
for Information Services—Permanence of Paper
for Printed Library Materials, ANSI Z39.48-1984.

Library of Congress Cataloging-in-Publication Data
Parsons, Paul F.
Inside America's Christian schools.

Includes index.
1. Church schools—United States. 2. Fundamentalist
churches—Education—United States.   I. Title.
LC531.P37 1987   377'.8'0973   87-24709
ISBN 0-86554-294-5 (alk. paper)

CONTENTS

To my parents,
Floyd and Christina Parsons,
who authored the author.

ACKNOWLEDGMENTS

This project was conceived during an evening with friends. David and Beverly McCollum casually mentioned seeing an advertisement for a Program in Religious Studies for Journalists, sponsored by the University of North Carolina at Chapel Hill. The idea intrigued me. As an editor with the Associated Press at the time, I was captivated with the thought of spending four months on a single project. And I had a topic in mind—the emergence of Christian schools in the United States.

The five of us who were named fellows in 1983 became a mutual support group. The religion faculty at the University of North Carolina served as a resource group. John Schutz, as program director, coordinated topical discussions for us, and his assistant, Jeanne Chamberlin, served as our troubleshooter. The Rockefeller Foundation provided funding for the program.

In the research itself, which ended up spanning four years rather than just that initial four months, I am indebted to the Christian school principals, teachers and students who let me visit their schools and ask intrusive questions—with only a promise on my part that I would do my best to be fair. In the writing, I am indebted to many scholars in both education and religion who commented on various drafts of the manuscript. For publication, I am indebted to the R. M. Seaton Endowment Fund at Kansas State University for financial support.

But I am most grateful to my wife, Mary Helen, who endured with a smile the arduous years of researching and writing. Thanks, all.

Paul F. Parsons
R. M. Seaton Professional Journalist Chair
Kansas State University

INTRODUCTION

Julie, a smart but increasingly rebellious teenager, glared at the spare schoolroom with nothing in it but a chair. In a disciplinary move born out of frustration, the school principal had sent her to an isolation room for talking back to a teacher.

"We put her in the room by herself, gave her a Bible and told her to read Proverbs," the principal recalled. "She didn't read any that morning because she was so mad at the world. But before the day was over, she decided she'd rather read than just sit there. She read the book of Proverbs and really broke. The spirit of God really dealt with her. God got ahold of her life that day."

Julie's days of teenage rebelliousness abruptly ended in an isolation room at a Christian school.

I related the story to some friends in Missouri. The wife beamed and said, "Isn't that wonderful! We hope we'll be able to find a good Christian school like that for our daughters." A few weeks later, I related the same story in the same way to a colleague from Rhode Island. His reply: "Isn't that scary! It reminds me of punitive isolation used on prison inmates years ago."

Same story. Opposite reactions. The Christian school movement tends to generate such polarization, even among the religious.

That's why I decided to write this book. Curiosity. At times, I'd hear people talk about the "godless public schools" and how they were thankful they had found a Christian school for their children. At other times, I'd hear people talk about those "racist academies" and those "Bible-thumper schools." I grew curious.

As a reporter for United Press International and then as an editor with the Associated Press from 1975 to 1983, I often wondered what these Christian schools were really like. The opportunity to satisfy my curiosity eventually came, thanks to a Program in Religious Studies for Journalists fellowship that gave me the freedom to investigate these schools nation-wide.

The sheer numbers alone came as a surprise. One of every eight schoolchildren in America today attends a private school.[1] More than one million of them go to fundamentalist and evangelical Christian schools—by far the fastest-growing segment in public or private education today. Conservatively, an estimated 15,000 of the schools exist nationwide. In the late 1970s and early 1980s, up to 1,000 Christian schools were starting in the United States each year. That frenetic pace of three new schools a day is believed to have slowed in the latter 1980s, but Christian schools remain in a period of expansion.[2]

The Christian school movement represents a quiet revolution within this nation's educational structure. While public school enrollment declined and Catholic school enrollment kept sliding, thousands of Christian schools started with little fanfare, many in church buildings that used to sit empty on weekdays. Churches that once offered only a Sunday School began pro-viding a Monday-through-Friday school as well.

Schools that bear the name ''Christian'' emerged shortly after World War II, but their years of dramatic growth have come since 1970—cor-responding with a conservative religious revival in the United States. Of course, schools with a religious emphasis have existed for a long time. Catholics established a parochial school system a century ago, and a few Protestant denominations such as the Lutherans, Episcopalians, and (Dutch) Christian Reformed also have long-established denominational schools.[3]

But a distinctly different type of religious school has arisen in recent years. These newly formed, and primarily fundamentalist, schools go by such names as New Testament Christian School, Grace 'N Glory Christian

---

[1]The U.S. Department of Education reports that 12.7% of all schoolchildren in the United States attended private schools in 1984-1985. This compares with 10.0% in 1975-1976 and 11.5% in 1980-1981. The figures are contained in the department's ''Digest of Education Statistics, 1985-1986.''

[2]Since Christian schools are not required to report their existence, government agencies are unable to monitor their numbers. However, one enterprise alone—Accelerated Chris-tian Education Inc.—was starting almost two schools a day during the late 1970s and early 1980s.

[3]See Otto F. Kraushaar's *American Nonpublic Schools: Patterns of Diversity* (Balti-more: The Johns Hopkins University Press, 1972).

Academy, Voice of Pentecost Christian School, and Abundant Life Christian Academy.

What are these new Christian schools like?

To answer that question, I visited schools in thirty states ranging from Maine to California. From the heart of New York City to rural Idabel, Oklahoma. From a school that meets in a St. Louis church basement to one that meets in a former public school facility in Hartford, Connecticut. From a long-established Christian school near Philadelphia to a newly founded one in Manhattan, Kansas. From a twelve-grade school with just a few dozen pupils in Yuma, Arizona, to a counterpart with more than 2,000 students in Pensacola, Florida.

These new Christian schools differ from their parochial and denominational brethren in their evangelistic fervor to inculcate the faith not only in their own young but in those outside the church body. Many proudly call themselves fundamentalist schools. Others do not embrace the fundamentalist label—for instance, schools operated by charismatic churches—yet the theological orientation is similar. Still others that go by the name ''Christian school'' are evangelical in nature but not at all fundamentalist in orientation. This book deals with this broad range, although it is heavily oriented toward fundamentalist schools since those are in the majority.

By calling these schools ''Christian schools,'' I do not mean to imply that other religious schools may not be Christian in nature—although some on the fundamentalist end of the theological spectrum do have a tendency to appropriate the term ''Christian'' for themselves with the implication that those who do not share their theological orientation are not Christian. This implication has created resentment and even animosity among mainline Christians, which in turn has spilled over to their attitudes about the Christian school movement itself. As a result, the Christian school movement is a controversial topic even among self-professed Christians.

The Christian school movement is burgeoning, but its precise size and growth rate are unknown. Three Christian school associations exist, but many schools are so separatist that they belong to no group.[4] The research

---

[4]The Association of Christian Schools International, based in La Habra, California, serves 2,500 schools with about 420,000 students. ACSI supports a broad spectrum of doctrinal positions, from the fundamentalists to the moderates to the charismatics. The American Association of Christian Schools, formerly in Normal, Illinois, and now based in Fairfax, Virginia, serves 1,200 schools with 170,000 students. AACS attracts fundamen-

task is further complicated because many of the more fundamentalist schools refuse to report enrollment figures to any government agency. Nevertheless, the U.S. Department of Education reports that enrollment in non-Catholic, church-related schools increased from 561,000 students in 1970 to 1,329,000 students in 1980. More recently, the department's National Center for Education Statistics reported that enrollment in these schools increased another twenty-two percent between 1980 and 1983.[5] Not all of these schools fall under the Christian school banner, of course, but a large majority do.

The "Bible Belt" remains the leading geographic area for Christian schools. Education statistics show that enrollment in non-Catholic, church-related schools in the South increased 311 percent between 1970 and 1980. The Mid-Atlantic region recorded a 288 percent increase, the West Coast a ninety-nine percent increase, the North-Central states a sixty-one percent increase, the Midwest a forty-eight percent increase, and the Northeast a forty-seven percent increase.

In state-by-state enrollment figures compiled by the U.S. Department of Education, Florida led the nation with more than 130,000 students in these schools. California was second with 106,000 students. Sixteen states experienced at least a quadrupling in enrollment during the decade. They were Alaska, Arkansas, Delaware, Florida, Georgia, Kentucky, Louisiana, Maine, Maryland, Nevada, New Hampshire, North Carolina, South Carolina, Tennessee, West Virginia, and Wyoming. The movement isn't limited to the smaller and medium-sized states. Ohio, Pennsylvania and Texas all reported a doubling in enrollment.

What once was a Southern phenomenon in the 1960s—the segregationist academies that were quickly formed in the name of God—has spread nationwide.

This growing popularity of Christian schools inevitably raises the question of racism. Indisputably, racial prejudice served as a motive in the establishment of many "Christian" schools, especially in the South where

---

talist church-sponsored schools; charismatics are excluded from membership. Christian Schools International, based in Grand Rapids, Michigan, serves 400 schools with 80,000 students. As the oldest and most liberal of the associations, it primarily serves Christian Reformed schools and does not attract fundamentalist schools.

[5]The U.S. Department of Education compiled its most recent state-by-state listing of enrollments in non-Catholic, church-related schools in 1980. A survey sample estimate was compiled in 1983, and Dr. Vance Grant of the Education Department's Center for Statistics said another survey sample estimate of religious school enrollment would be released in the late 1980s.

the courts first began the process of dismantling a dual public school system. Yet it is simplistic to conclude that all Christian schools today are racially motivated. How could one explain the Christian school I visited in Newark, New Jersey, that has a 40 percent black enrollment? Or the pentecostal school I visited in Charlotte, North Carolina, where one of every eight students is black? Or the two Christian schools across the street from one another in Gulfport, Mississippi—both integrated? Or the all-black fundamentalist school I visited in Baton Rouge, Louisiana? Or the creation of Christian schools in nearly all-white communities?

ENROLLMENT IN NON-CATHOLIC RELIGIOUS SCHOOLS					
Compiled by the National Center for Education Statistics					
STATE	1970	1980	STATE	1970	1980
------------------- NORTHEAST -------------------			------------------ NORTH-CENTRAL ------------------		
Connecticut	3,890	5,639	Illinois	39,982	45,441
Maine	586	2,805	Indiana	15,040	29,564
Massachusetts	3,310	5,208	Kentucky	2,090	19,502
New Hampshire	680	3,596	Michigan	39,590	65,901
New Jersey	9,771	16,539	Ohio	9,942	26,175
New York	71,486	82,995	Wisconsin	38,330	46,287
Pennsylvania	21,569	47,713			
Rhode Island	2,012	2,217	---------------------- MIDWEST ----------------------		
Vermont	66	209	Iowa	6,770	9,095
			Kansas	2,394	4,765
------------------- MID-ATLANTIC -------------------			Minnesota	14,176	20,107
Delaware	1,074	8,649	Missouri	13,897	22,268
Maryland	9,362	38,279	Nebraska	5,281	7,038
Virginia	15,202	52,009	North Dakota	804	858
Washington DC	3,075	8,989	South Dakota	1,364	2,226
West Virginia	178	4,142			
			------------------------- WEST -------------------------		
------------------------ SOUTH ------------------------			Alaska	286	3,203
Alabama	37,836	47,949	Arizona	3,230	11,009
Arkansas	2,273	11,200	California	59,993	106,830
Florida	22,157	130,720	Colorado	5,173	10,749
Georgia	3,763	69,208	Hawaii	3,637	8,922
Louisiana	10,666	46,822	Idaho	1,617	3,273
Mississippi	10,903	38,774	Montana	902	2,059
North Carolina	4,378	48,755	Nevada	276	1,350
Oklahoma	3,721	8,954	New Mexico	2,017	3,637
South Carolina	10,231	42,064	Oregon	5,420	9,412
Tennessee	7,766	56,432	Utah	1,122	638
Texas	24,911	68,768	Washington	7,560	19,693
			Wyoming	49	889
TOTALS	1970: 561,808			1980: 1,329,526	

A study by two University of Wisconsin researchers concluded that the Christian school movement of today is motivated not so much by racial beliefs as by a growing desire to return to the values and disciplines of the past.[6] Just as fundamentalist churches emphasize "old-time religion," fundamentalist schools are emphasizing "old-time education." Still, Christian schooling is an overwhelmingly white phenomenon. That fact cannot be ignored.

The sole objective of this book is to provide insight into the Christian school movement—why it is happening, what the schools are like, and what their impact may be on the future of American education.

I am a journalist—a historian-in-a-hurry, so to speak. A journalist does not rely on the analysis of secondary data but instead creates new data through interviews and observation. Different research methodologies are applicable in different disciplines. Psychologists rely on independent observations for their data. Anthropologists rely on repeated observations of a group of people engaged in their customary activities. Historians typically turn to archives for published data.

Field notes are to journalists what archives are to historians—the primary sources of information without which no history could be written. My field notes serve as my primary sources of information. This means there is inescapable intrusion into the source material. I have my own personality, my own prejudices, my own way of seeing reality. Field notes, without doubt, are polluted. But we must start somewhere in developing a body of literature about these new Christian schools. This is an attempt to give a comprehensive overview of these schools, flawed as it may be in its dependence on one person's field notes.

For a journalist, the problem always is determining how much field work is enough to prevent spurious reportage. The answer really is quite simple. I stopped data-gathering when I began seeing in visits to Christian schools almost total repetition in philosophy, structure, and school atmosphere. That continuous repetition is a sign that a field researcher has gained not just a body of anecdotes, but significant information about a movement in general.

All illustrations in this book are true. All quotations are legitimate. All names, places, and titles are accurate, within the boundaries of the passage

---

[6]Virginia Davis Nordin and William Lloyd Turner, "More Than Segregation Academies: The Growing Protestant Fundamentalist Schools," *Phi Delta Kappan* (February 1980): 391-94.

of time from the visits to the printed page. Since research spanned four years and publication required another year, some of the persons named in this book may no longer be in the same positions of responsibility. Their titles and institutional affiliations, as published, represent their roles of responsibility at the time of the school visits. Admittedly, retracing the author's footsteps to ascertain accuracy is not as simple in a field study as in an archival study. But the information in this book is not disguised behind pseudonyms or anonymity.

This book has a modest goal—to inform. Its goal is not to persuade or to argue or to judge. This is not, then, a book that emphasizes the traditional scholarly order of argument, evidence, analysis, and illustration. So when I permit a comment from a source to stand unchallenged—for instance, those in Christian schooling tend to portray the public schools in sweeping brushstrokes of black and blue—it does not mean I necessarily agree with the comment. I let the comment stand on its own because this is not a book in which I am trying to prove a point. My purpose is to let readers gain insight into the perspective of those in the forefront of the Christian school movement and gain insight into what these new schools are like. The book relies heavily on the anecdotal style because there is no better way than illustration to get a glimpse inside these schools.

The school visits occurred between 1983 and 1986. Some schools were visited by design. I wanted to visit Jerry Falwell's junior high school in Virginia, I wanted to observe the Christian school founded by Tim LaHaye in San Diego, and I wanted to tour the fundamentalist Bob Jones Academy in South Carolina. Other schools were selected on a spot basis. I mapped out an itinerary and selected schools to visit on the basis of phone books, Christian school directories and conversations. I sought a balance between the self-instructional fundamentalist schools and the traditional-classroom schools.

Fundamentalist schools, in particular, operate in secrecy. This is done not only to discourage the prying of government agencies but to avoid the eyeing of a suspicious public. Knowing this, I made sure some of my visits to Christian schools were unannounced. I simply would arrive at a school at 8 a.m. and introduce myself to the understandably wary principal. After explaining my purpose, not once was I turned away. On showing up without notice at a Christian academy in rural North Carolina, the principal was amazed I had heard of the school, much less found it. "Our school is only for our church members' children," he said. "Most of the community around here doesn't even know we exist." The school wasn't listed in the phone book, nor was there a sign outside. I had found a reference to it in a directory of Christian schools and had spent the preceding afternoon on the North Carolina backroads searching for it.

Other visits were scheduled in advance. Twice I was told over the phone that I could not come. The rejections came from schools in Alabama and Mississippi. When it happened the first time, my reporter instinct was aroused. When in the South at a later date, I made a side trip to the Christian school in Alabama where the principal had politely told me that his school board president didn't like "snoops." When I entered his office and introduced myself, the principal looked at me in surprise, then amusement. "Well," the principal said, "you wanted to officially set up a visit and I had to ask you not to come. But now that you're just a pop-in visitor, let me show you around." He let me visit the school without hindrance. The other rejection came from the principal of a fundamentalist school in Biloxi, Mississippi. He told me on the phone: "Brother, I'm sorry, but I don't let anybody but the children and their parents inside this school. I don't even let my curriculum company know how many kids we've got." I would discover in the course of research that this view stems from repeated battles with government agencies in some states.

The fact that I received only two rejections in visits to Christian schools in thirty states doesn't mean the others welcomed me with open arms. I had to make repeated overtures to officials at Bob Jones University before gaining less-than-enthusiastic permission to visit their junior high and high school academies. This strict fundamentalist school was stripped in 1983 of its tax-exempt status by the Internal Revenue Service for having a policy that prohibits blacks and whites from dating or marrying. "We get a lot of bad press," a school official said in an understatement. It also required tenacity to get inside the elementary school run by Pensacola Christian in Florida. Once there, a school official stayed with me the entire day, never letting me out of sight. Still, these difficult-to-obtain visits gave me insight into the breadth and depth of the diverse Christian school movement.

In the pages to follow, you'll be introduced to the philosophy behind these schools and discover why fundamentalists consider the public schools to be a godless educational system.

You'll learn that these schools have their own moralizing textbooks and even their own Christian dictionary. Hair-length codes and paddlings are common. And just as important as reading and 'riting is the teaching of right and 'rong.

You'll learn that boys in fundamentalist schools are taught to be the head of the household and girls are taught to be helpmates, that Darwin's theory of evolution is considered "unscientific," and that many fundamentalists believe an emphasis on competitive sports produces shallow, superficial Christians.

You'll discover that not all is rosy for the Christian school movement. There is a public perception that all Christian schools are racist academies. There is a never-ending battle between fundamentalists and the government over just who is in charge of these schools. There is occasional discord within the authoritarian structures of these schools as well.

Finally, we'll look at the future of the Christian school movement. Can education exist apart from religion? Is the Christian school movement a temporary phenomenon, or has our unique 150-year-old public school experiment forever failed in the eyes of conservative Christians? Is the creation of a network of Christian schools an example of American pluralism at its best, even though these schools may shun pluralism in favor of religious separatism? These are some of the questions at the heart of this study of the Christian school movement.

Because this book seeks to inform rather than to argue, it is written with many audiences in mind.

As a parent, you may be wrestling with problems in your local public schools. You find yourself wondering about these Christian schools that seem to emphasize what you want emphasized—discipline, moral values, and back-to-basics academics.

As a citizen, you may be struggling to reconcile the Christian school movement with your long-held beliefs that a free, public education is the backbone of democracy. You find yourself questioning the motives of those who find it so convenient to withdraw their children from the public schools instead of staying to solve the problems that exist.

As a taxpayer, you may be debating the merits of tuition tax credits for parents who send their children to private schools. You find yourself either fiercely for or against the concept, and hoping to receive validation for your views.

As a conservative Christian, you may already be sold on the value of Christian schools. You find yourself curious to see how an observer from outside the movement views the academic integrity of these schools.

As a college student majoring in education, you may be intrigued at the job opportunities resulting from the explosive growth of Christian schools. You find yourself wondering if you'd fit in as a teacher at one of these schools.

Or as a scholar, or public school teacher, or parent whose children are not yet school age, you simply may be curious about this quiet revolution in American education. You find yourself wanting to know the purpose of the movement, what the schools are like, and what their impact may be on society.

The mere mention of religious schools once brought a vision of nuns clad in the traditional habit. No more. Many Protestant parents, who a decade ago looked down on private schools as luxuries for the rich or the Roman Catholic, have done an about-face. Now, parents who can barely meet their mortgage payments are viewing Christian academies as educational necessities.

The dramatic increase in Christian schools in the United States is one of the more significant educational phenomena of the decade. I hope this book will provide you insight into this phenomenon.

THE MISSION: PROVIDING A BIBLICAL HOTHOUSE

I grew up in Oregon, and we had a hothouse nearby to grow tomatoes during the winter months. Outside the door were scrawny, gnarled plants that didn't make it inside the hot-house. They were handicapped. Inside, the tomatoes were healthy and strong. The Christian school movement per-forms that function. It gets some basic character established before the child does battle with the world.

Dr. Paul A. Kienel
Association of Christian Schools International
La Habra, California

1

MORE
THAN ACADEMICS—
A LIFESTYLE

Somewhat noisily, 350 teenagers
streamed into the school gymnasium and settled into folding chairs for the
weekly chapel service. Once it quietened, the school administrator sum-
moned a fifteen-year-old named John out of the crowd and asked him to
take a seat on the front row. The principal then read Proverbs 27:5, which
says: "Open rebuke is better than concealed love."

Eyes widened. Teenagers exchanged sidewise glances. The squeaking
of folding chairs abruptly ceased. The moment belonged to Paul E. Young,
administrator of the Southern Baptist Educational Complex in Memphis,
Tennessee.

"Two weeks ago," the principal told the now-alert teens, "John brought to school a marijuana cigarette and showed it to his friends. This is something we will not stand for. The first response of the school board was to expel him. But the need is to minister to him, to help him break this habit. He has pledged to do so. I hope God is convicting him in his own heart right now."

John sat motionless on the front row, facing Young. He and his parents had been apprised in advance of the planned rebuke.

"Not only is John guilty," Young continued, his voice softening, "but you—his peers—are guilty and I am guilty for concealing our love for him. People like John who are searching for acceptance are really seeking love. Now, you could rebuke us for doing this to him. But John was led to the Lord by another student in our weight room a few years ago, and we are following the scripture that says we are to rebuke sin. John, we hate the sin you are involved in, but we love you."

Back in his office, Young shared with me his struggle in deciding to put John through the trauma of an open rebuke in front of his peers.

"There are some people on our school board who want us to teach Bible, Bible, Bible, Bible. Some believe we should be an all-day Sunday School. But we have children who are really gospel-hardened, like John. He said he's a Christian, but his conduct didn't reflect it. Now here's a guy in a Christian environment all the time, and he was smoking marijuana every day after school. He started when he was eight. I told my board if we kick him out, we'll never have an opportunity to reach him. But we also have a responsibility to our other students to let them know we're not going to accept this behavior. We thought the open rebuke was one way of doing that."

An open rebuke based on a Bible verse is not your everyday occurrence at school. But then, Christian schools operate on a different standard from public schools. Christian schools can begin classes with prayer. They can require students to memorize Bible verses. They can teach the creation account in Genesis. In short, as a private form of education, these schools not only can teach the three R's but are free to emphasize the fourth R as well—religion.

Religious instruction, obviously, is a common denominator in all Christian schools. Walk into a first-grade class at Riverdale Baptist School in Maryland and you will hear the six-year-olds reciting, in unison, lengthy passages from the Gospel of John. Sit in the twelfth-grade Bible class at Barrington Christian Academy in Rhode Island and you will gain an overview of religious cults in America. Visit the weekly chapel service at the

Paw Creek Christian Academy in Charlotte, North Carolina, and you will hear the pastor's dispensational premillennialist view of the end of time. Step inside a history class at Christian High School in El Cajon, California, and you will hear teenagers beginning class with a prayer for the president.

Another common denominator is the maintaining of a strict regimentation. Paddlings are common, punctuality is emphasized, and respect for adults is shown through standard ''yes ma'ams'' and ''no sirs.'' Back talk to a teacher is a serious offense. At some schools, students are instructed to stand whenever an adult enters the room. Boys who go to fundamentalist schools have the shortest hair in town. Girls have a closet full of dresses since pants and jeans are taboo at most of these schools.

These common threads of religious instruction and strict regimentation are woven within a fabric of academic diversity. More than 5,000 fundamentalist schools have embarked on a bold experiment in a ''teacherless'' classroom. The philosophy is that students learn best by working out of a book at their own speed rather than by sitting in a teacher-led classroom that proceeds at the pace of the average child. More than 5,000 other Christian schools go the conventional route, with a teacher at the blackboard and twenty or so pupils at their desks.

Christian schools in both academic camps tend to shun the state-adopted textbooks found in public schools. Instead, they use books published expressly for them. In these books, history is the tracing of the fingerprints of God through time. Science is a study of creation, with just enough evolutionary theory tossed in for students to be able to refute it. Even the math books carry examples with a message. One math problem reads: ''Kimberly received $10.00 for her birthday. She gave $1.50 in Sunday School, spent $3.98 on a new purse and put the rest in her savings account. How much did she put in her savings account?'' Not only should the children come up with the answer of $4.52, but they see Kimberly as a role model who is generous to the church—giving fifteen percent instead of the traditional ten percent tithe—and who saves her remaining money rather than spending it frivolously.

Christian schools do not have students immersed in the Bible seven hours a day. Students are taught social studies, grammar, arithmetic, history, and the rest just as in the public schools. A history teacher at a Christian school in rural North Carolina said: ''I don't believe that all we ought to do is read the Bible. The Lord gave us minds to develop. We're to produce mature young people who are committed to renewing their own minds.'' The Bible, then, isn't the only book opened during a school day. But it does serve as the focal point for all subjects. Christian schools want an academic environment, yes; but they place the need for a religious environment on a higher pedestal. Christian schools bathe every academic subject in scripture. All of learning is approached from a moralistic point of view. No dividing line exists between academics and religion because Christian schools consider the two inseparably linked.

"We encourage the integration of biblical principles," a Christian school principal in California said. "In a geometry class, you won't find teachers banging on the Bible. But the bulletin boards on the walls show geometry in nature. God is shown as the creator of the universe. It gives the student a different perspective on lines and planes."

Few Christian schools claim to have all of the resources available in the public schools. Many lack the impressive science labs, or the computer classes, or the audiovisual equipment. Some do not have extras such as a marching band, a football team, or a school newspaper. But these Christian schools claim to offer a type of education they say the public schools ignore—a moral education.

Illustration: A high school graduate wrote a letter of apology to the principal at Calumet Christian School in Gary, Indiana. She said she had come to Calumet as an "A" student from a public school, where she had cheated. She wrote: "I brought the habit with me. Calumet was so tough that I kept on cheating. There were times I'd sit in Chapel with such deep convictions of doing wrong. Please forgive me." The young woman was now in college, preparing for missions work. "It's good to know the seeds were planted," the school principal said. "That's what a Christian education is all about."

The short-term purpose of these rapidly multiplying schools is to give the youth a moral as well as an academic education. The long-term purpose is ultimately to change the state and health of the Republic. Conservative Christians view society as sick and view the public schools as agents of sickness. They believe the only way to turn America around is to return to the values and disciplines in the Bible. Instead of working for change from the bottom up within the prevailing system, they are fleeing society's basic institutions such as the public schools in order to train their young in their own way. The intent is for these children to return one day to society's basic institutions and transform America from the top down.

This training to be part of God's army begins early in life.

Christian school consultant Reggie Sellers spoke in a hushed voice as second graders paraded two-by-two down a hallway at Pensacola Christian School in Florida. He whispered: "You cannot separate God from education. Why does $2 + 2 = 4$? It's because God put order in the universe."

Talking isn't permitted in the hallway. Instead, the teacher gives hand signals to start and stop the line of children. "We have a big school and the kids know they can't be noisy," Sellers said. "We're teaching more than academics here. We're teaching a Christian lifestyle."

Sellers and I rounded a corner and reached an intersection of hallways. A long line of children silently walking two-by-two toward the cafeteria dissected our path. I slowed, but Sellers kept walking so I stayed with him. Sure enough, just like the waters of the Red Sea parting for Moses, the line of children parted just as we reached it, with the preceding twosomes walking on and the succeeding twosomes coming to a perfectly timed halt to let us through without one step's delay. Not a word had been spoken. The hallway was quiet except for the soft patter of shoes. We walked on, and I couldn't help but glance back in amazement. The two parts of the line had reunited by now, in straight rows that would make a drill sergeant proud.

I had heard about this school from a Christian school principal in another state. He had told me: "Very structured. You stand to answer in a classroom. Hands in lap in class. You walk down the hall on a certain side. The middle of the hall is for the principal, and you don't want to bump into the principal!"

Pensacola Christian is one of the largest fundamentalist schools in the nation. The elementary school alone has more than 1,300 students. The school hums like a well-oiled machine. Classes coming from and going to the cafeteria are all orderly, properly timed and quiet.

It's the same inside the cafeteria. The only sounds come from forks scraping plates and an occasional squeak from a chair. Pupils in kindergarten through third grade can't talk in the cafeteria. "If they're talking, they're not eating," Sellers said. "They are in the cafeteria to eat." Pupils in the fourth grade and above are allowed to talk the final ten minutes of the lunch break if they have finished eating. Boys sit on one side of the table; girls on the other.

Walking down the long, immaculately kept hallways, you hear students reviewing phonics lessons in unison. In the classrooms pupils read from modern McGuffey Readers that have a moral to every story.

In a third-grade classroom, carpeted and colorful with the American and Christian flags in the corner, the teacher instructs the class on the intricacies of multiplication. Pupils raise their hands to be called on. No child blurts out an answer. And when called on by the teacher, the children stand to give the answer. In a kindergarten class, the teacher draws a chicken on the blackboard and tells the children that a chicken has only three toes. The twenty-nine kids giggle; the teacher smiles. A 29-to-1 ratio—and this teacher is blessed. The schoolwide ratio is 34-to-1. "If the teacher maintains discipline, the teacher-pupil ratio doesn't matter," Sellers said.

This is certainly a school that maintains discipline. The school, in fact, is eerily quiet. Children know the rules, and they know they either obey the rules or get in trouble.

Across the continent, in southern California, is a very different type of Christian school. At Christian High School in El Cajon, where classes are rather noisy by comparison, teacher Dean Conk starts each of his academic Bible classes with prayer. Students readily offer prayer requests for themselves, their families, and friends. The lesson that day, from Philippians, deals with rejoicing in the Lord no matter what the circumstances of life. Conk reminds the class that the Apostle Paul had written the message to the church at Philippi while in prison. "Paul wasn't lying on the beach in Palm Springs, sipping through a straw, and writing a letter," Conk said. "He was writing from a difficult circumstance, yet he was still rejoicing in the Lord. We make our God into a little wimp sometimes. So powerless. We say, 'Well, he can't handle *my* problem.' Oh, yes, he can."

"Bible" is a required course for students attending Christian High. A student may have Geometry during first period, Spanish during second period, Bible during third period, American History during fourth period, and so on. For students, the Bible course is a combination of inspiration and perspiration. The perspiration consists of memorizing Bible verses for credit or learning details about the Apostle Paul's missionary journeys. Students read and study large portions of the Bible for class credit. Amid this academic intent, however, Conk aims for inspiration as well. His lectures are aimed at getting students to think about their reason for existing.

Using the passage in Philippians as a starting point, Conk this day tells the teenagers that each of them needs a purpose in life. "You say, 'My purpose is to go to heaven.' Well and good. But do you have personal goals? Something to achieve during your life? Set goals for yourself and then meet them," Conk said. The teacher also advised students to make sure their actions match their claims of being born again. "Don't tell people you're a Christian if there's no evidence," he said. "I don't pump weights and I don't claim to. I don't have the evidence of doing so. In this country, 133 million people call themselves Christians, but we don't have 133 million people acting like it."

At lunch, I joined a group of teenagers munching sandwiches and talking on typical topics such as the coming weekend or the fast-approaching history test. Later, I talked with a seventeen-year-old named Dan, the son of a missionary who served in Iran until forced out in 1980. Dan regularly meets with twenty other students during lunch in a voluntary prayer session. He likes going to a school that bills itself as having a Christian environment. "When you're in a public school and the others know you're a Christian, they're always watching to see if you goof up," Dan said. "Here, everyone takes it for granted that you're a Christian. The pressure is off."

Between Pensacola with its quiet hallways and El Cajon with its student prayer groups are thousands of other Christian schools—all different, all distinctive. Some are large, some small. Some are fundamentalist, some aren't. Some are expensive, some not. Some meet in churches, some in abandoned public school buildings. Some teach church doctrine, some avoid it. Some are segregated, some integrated. They often have little in common except the name "Christian school" and what that implies.

And just what does that imply? Without exception, it implies that more than academics is taught here—that the teaching of a lifestyle is in progress as well. The Christian school movement considers its primary mission to be the teaching of a lifestyle during the impressionable, growing-up years.

At Jerry Falwell's Christian academy in Lynchburg, Virginia, administrator Glen Schultz says the growing-up years are just naturally traumatic. "Whether they are Christian or not, kids aren't perfect," he said. "We deal with kids with the same problems as anyone. The difference is, we're giving them direction spiritually."

A West Virginia school administrator estimates that a third of his students are strong Christians, a third aren't, and the other third are in the middle. "The good kids are battling the bad kids for the middle-of-the-road kids," said Edward Davis, principal of the Martinsburg Christian Academy.

Fundamentalists, in particular, take spiritual warfare very seriously. They view life as a constant tug-of-war between good and evil, light and darkness, right and wrong. All of life is cast in absolutist terms, and they operate their schools with this uncompromising view.

Of the roughly 15,000 Christian schools in America, the vast majority proudly wear the fundamentalist label.

Calvary Baptist Christian School in Keokuk, Iowa, is an example of a fundamentalist school. Its students follow strict hair and dress codes. They wear red-white-and-blue uniforms. They are prohibited from playing video games, from dating, from going coed swimming, and even from driving on Keokuk's Main Street—a barhopper's delight in this small Mississippi River town. Established in the mid-1970s, the school is sponsored by an independent Baptist church whose pastor serves as the school superintendent. Tuition is under one hundred dollars a month per child. The school is small, with thirty-nine students in kindergarten through twelfth grade. Most pupils are children of church members. Because of its size, the school uses Accelerated Christian Education's "teacherless" curriculum. Each school discussion is cast in a biblical framework that follows specific church doctrine. None of the adult supervisors in the school are state certified. In fact, the pastor told me with a note of pride in his voice: "Technically speaking, we do not have a single qualified teacher in our school." Other than the principal and one other paid worker, the staff consists of volunteer mothers. Graduating seniors, if they go to college, usually attend Bible schools and not state universities.

Not all Christian schools, however, are fundamentalist. Lexington Christian Academy near Boston is an example of a nonfundamentalist Christian school. The atmosphere is much like a public school. The mood is casual. Boys have longer hair; girls wear jeans and T-shirts with slogans. Students don't address teachers with the deferential respect found in the fundamentalist schools. The school is parent operated, not church operated, and draws its 251 high school students from 120 churches and seventeen denominations. The principal told me: "We major on the majors and don't delve into doctrine. The end result, hopefully, will be the development of a thoughtful person who will be able to seek his own revelation from God." The school uses the same textbooks found in public schools. Sometimes God is a topic in class; sometimes not, depending on the subject matter. Tuition is about $4,000 a year. The school is accredited and fully cooperates with government agencies. The teaching corps is highly educated, and eighty-eight percent of the graduating seniors go to college, including Ivy League schools. This type of Christian school is like an elite public school sprinkled with holy water.

A fundamentalist school, though, is dramatically different. One fundamentalist academy in South Carolina doesn't allow teenage boys and girls to walk together unescorted on the school grounds. A school in Des Moines considers television so evil that it refuses to enroll a child until mom and dad get rid of the family TV set. A school in Arizona requires the child and at least one parent to go to church four times a week—to Sunday School, to the Sunday morning worship service, to the Sunday night worship service and to the Wednesday night prayer meeting. A school in Maine considers the 1611 King James Version to be the only valid translation of scripture. A school in Arkansas so dislikes Halloween, with its witches-and-ghosts motif, that it sponsors a dress-up day in late October when elementary children come as Bible characters such as Moses, John the Baptist, and Mary.

To understand fundamentalist Christian schools, one needs to understand the fundamentalist perspective. Fundamentalism represents a strict adherence to Christian doctrines based on a literal interpretation of the Bible. Fundamentalists believe in the infallability of the Bible, the virgin birth and divinity of Jesus Christ, the atoning power of his crucifixion, his bodily resurrection, and his eventual second coming. They oppose the accommodation of Christian doctrine to modern scientific theory and philosophy. Their worldview is that God not only created the universe and created humankind, but that God created absolute rules under which society should operate. These absolutes are to be ascertained through reading the Bible and through prayer.

The roots of fundamentalism lie in the basic doctrines of biblical inerrancy and millennialism—the belief that the Bible is inspired by God and without error and the belief that Christ will physically return to establish a 1,000-year earthly reign. These two doctrines gained strength in Protestantism in the mid- to late-1800s.

The term "fundamentalist" came into vogue when sixty-four scholars and preachers concerned with the infiltration of modernism in churches published a series of twelve pamphlets entitled "The Fundamentals." The pamphlets, published between 1910 and 1915, attacked theories of biblical criticism and reasserted the authority of the Bible. In the 1920s, theological differences between liberals and fundamentalists led to separations in many of the established churches of the day. Between then and World War II, and to a minor degree since then, there have been a series of departures from the mainline denominations.[1]

Ironically, a 1941 work by the theologically liberal H. Shelton Smith is cited by fundamentalists for opening their eyes to the need for Christian schools. In his book *Faith and Nurture,* Smith concluded that humanism was an established religion in the public schools and was at war with the religion of the churches. While testifying in a Christian school court case in North Carolina, modern-day fundamentalist philosopher Rousas Rushdoony told the court: "Many of the men who established the first of the fundamentalist schools have told me that they were influenced by that

---

[1]Among the books that define the character of the fundamentalist movement and describe its origins are Stewart G. Cole's *The History of Fundamentalism* (Hamden CT: Anchor Books, 1931), Ernest R. Sandeen's *The Roots of Fundamentalism: British and American Millenarianism, 1800-1930* (Chicago: University of Chicago Press, 1970), and George M. Marsden's *Fundamentalism and American Culture: The Shaping of Twentieth-Century Evangelicalism, 1870-1925* (New York: Oxford University Press, 1980).

statement. It opened their eyes that their separation had been incomplete to that day, and so—in terms of their faith—they had to continue the separation. As a result, there is a growing self-consciousness within the fundamentalist movement. As they make one stand, it leads to the implication that this stand must lead to further stands."[2]

These stands have progressively led fundamentalists into greater conflict with societal change. First came the battle with modernism in the churches, then skepticism in the evolutionary sciences, and now humanism in the public schools and liberalism in politics.

To fundamentalists, society is deteriorating and nothing can change that fact except Jesus' return to earth. In the meantime, they consider it their responsibility to evangelize as much of the world as possible. Fundamentalists take personal salvation seriously. They anguish over someone who is "lost" and not "born again."

This evangelistic thrust is evident in the Christian schools. A fourth-grade teacher at a Christian school in Tennessee has a personal goal that no child go through the year without being confronted with the salvation message. One day her husband came home from work and found her in the bedroom, crying. Asked what was the matter, she replied, "There's one little boy in my class that I just can't seem to reach spiritually." Before the year was over, the teacher succeeded in leading him to make a profession of faith in Jesus Christ.

This illustration isn't at all unusual. The Association of Christian Schools International reported in 1986 that 30,000 students at its member schools had been converted during the preceding academic year. In sharing that statistic with member schools, the association said in its newsletter: "Evangelism should be a normal part of the everyday curriculum in 'God's school system.' How tragic it would be if a non-Christian student were to attend a Christian school without once being invited to receive Jesus Christ."[3]

The intent of Christian schooling, then, is not just to develop the mind, but to correspondingly influence the very souls of its students.

---

[2]Rushdoony's testimony in State of North Carolina v. Columbus Christian Academy, Wake County Superior Court, 5 September 1978.

[3]Paul Kienel, "Evangelism in Christian Schools," *Christian School Comment* (January 1986): 1.

2

SHELTERING KIDS
FROM
THE WORLD

Across the nation, supporters and critics alike compare the Christian school to a hothouse.

"You have to realize the purpose of a hothouse," says Dr. Paul A. Kienel, executive director of the Association of Christian Schools International. "A hothouse is designed to protect young, tender plants during their growing years so they can be transplanted in the real world later on and be ahead of plants that didn't have the opportunity.

"I grew up in Oregon, and we had a hothouse nearby to grow tomatoes during the winter months. Outside the door were scrawny, gnarled plants that didn't make it inside the hothouse. They were handicapped. Inside, the tomatoes were healthy and strong. The Christian school movement performs that function. It gets some basic character established before the child does battle with the world.''

Critics warn, however, that too much of a hothouse life can lead to "root rot." When asked one day where she went to school, a little girl in Knoxville, Tennessee, straightened up in her chair and said with seriousness: "I go to a Christian school. There's no sin there!''

Students who attend the Christian school hothouses across America seem to be there by choice. I talked privately with hundreds of students, mostly on the secondary level, and found little resentment for either the hothouse aspect or the strict discipline. Some would just as soon be back in a public school because of a more diverse curriculum or because that's where many of their friends are. But most unequivocally say the decision to go to a Christian school was theirs.

This overwhelmingly positive reaction from students is a product of the enrollment process at these schools. Some churches operate hothouses only for the children of their own members. Others view Christian schools as evangelistic ministries, and these school leaders proudly tell of converting to their belief system the children of Hindus, Mormons, Catholics, and atheists.

Seldom does a Christian school turn away a student because of IQ. A few schools test children and take only those on grade level or above. But these are the exceptions rather than the rule. Selectivity usually is not based on brainpower. "We aren't a brain factory," one Christian school principal in California said. "Some kids have four-cylinder brains and some have eight-cylinder brains. Our commitment is to the Christian home, so if the four-cylinder kids operate on all four cylinders, we accept them."[1]

Rather than brainpower, the selection process more often is tied to a student's attitude. Before accepting a student, many principals interview both the parents and child—separately. If the child doesn't want to go to the school, that's usually an automatic rejection slip to the parents. Christian schools don't want rebels.

Michael Healan, principal of Hartford Christian Academy in Connecticut, interviews every prospective student individually from the fifth grade on up. Recently, he interviewed a seventh grade boy whose parents wanted him to go to the Christian school. "I told the parents to leave," Healan said, "and then I explained our rules and asked the boy if he wanted

---

[1] "The Bright Flight," *Newsweek* (20 April 1981): 73.

to come here. He said, 'No sir, I don't want to be here.' So I called the parents back in and said no.'' Later, Healan interviewed an eighth grader who did want to come. ''The boy said he was facing lots of temptations at his public school,'' Healan said. ''He said kids were constantly pressuring him to take drugs and do things he didn't want to do. At that age, some don't have a character strong enough to withstand peer pressure. They are tender young plants who can't take the storms of life yet.''

Fifteen-year-old Shawn had been dismissed from Christian High in El Cajon because he was a constant discipline problem. Shawn spent a year back in a public school. He's since returned to Christian High—at his request. He said he had come to appreciate the discipline and atmosphere of a Christian school.

Conversely, sixteen-year-old Jim has been in a Christian school since the second grade. He didn't want to come then, and he doesn't particularly like being in one now. ''I still resist some,'' he told me while exchanging books at his school locker in Gary, Indiana. My friends are there, and it's got some advanced science courses I'd like to take. But I'm not the age yet where I can go against my parents' wishes. So I'll stay and tough it out.''

In New York, a high school student named José said he first came to a Christian school at the age of ten. He returned to the public schools for awhile, but switched back. ''In the public schools,'' José said, ''I was just another number. They don't care about your spiritual life. Here they really care for you.'' José says it would be tough to remain spiritual as a teenager in a public school in New York City. ''It's possible, I guess, but I don't know if I'd be strong enough.''

Many students say their satisfaction with their Christian school stems from the home-style attitude of the teachers. ''The teachers here care for you,'' said a ninth grader in Charlotte, North Carolina. ''In the public school I went to, if you were having problems, the teacher would say, 'Do you want to go home?' They didn't really care. Here, the teacher pulls you aside and tries to find out what's the matter.''

Teachers in America's fundamentalist schools are an unusual group indeed. Some are volunteers. Those who get a paycheck receive, on the whole, atrocious salaries.

A few Christian schools—mostly the nonfundamentalist ones—do pay competitive salaries. Christian Life Academy in Baton Rouge waits for the local school board to set public school teacher salaries for the following year and then adopts the same salary schedule. But a salary schedule comparable to the public sector is atypical. The Illinois Association of Christian Schools surveyed its schools in 1982-1983 and found the median teacher salary at schools with more than 200 students to be $9,295 a year. At schools with fewer than 200 students, the median salary was $8,230 a year.[2]

An Alabama principal says he is compensated spiritually instead of financially. An Iowa principal adds: "If I can train children to walk in the ways of the Lord, heaven is where I'll get my big salary." On earth, he made $9,000 a year.

One should not underestimate this hidden factor in the Christian school movement: Many teachers actually view their work as a ministry instead of as a job. As a result, it is impossible to look at teacher salaries and say with precision that you get what you pay for.

Salaries, though, remain a touchy issue. A Rhode Island principal spotted a pamphlet from another Christian school that told parents tuition is kept low because teachers consider their work a ministry. "I blew my top," he said. "They have no right to make that a publicity point. I wouldn't dare hire someone and tell them I wasn't going to pay them much because it should be a ministry to them. That's a distortion of scripture. Low salaries in Christian schools is a valid perception now, but let's not legislate that perception."

Students say they recognize and appreciate the sacrifices, both financial and personal, that their teachers make. A twelfth grader at Martinsburg Christian Academy in West Virginia said teachers have come to his home in the evenings to tutor him for free when he's having trouble with schoolwork. He said he's never heard of a public school teacher doing that. A sophomore at the school added: "Look, I know the teachers aren't here for the money. That makes me respect them even more."

A special bond exists between teacher and student in these schools. Teachers seem genuinely concerned about the academic progress and moral development of their students. Students also know that if they don't behave or do their work, the teacher and the parent will communicate. After all, the parent is paying out of the pocket for this education.

Christian schools view the task of education as a joint venture between parent and school. Here is the story of Sandy, a fifteen-year-old Hispanic who attended Manhattan Christian Academy in New York City. The school itself is housed in an old brick building spray-painted with graffiti on the outside. Trash collects in the gutter out front. At recess, kids climb on the

---

[2]"Tuition, Salary and Benefit Survey," *The Administrator,* a quarterly publication of the American Association of Christian Schools (Winter 1983): 16.

fire hydrant or play kickball in the middle of 205th Street, which the police each day barricade for one block to create a playground. Inside, principal David Whitaker bubbled with enthusiasm. The twelve-grade A.C.E. school is ninety percent Hispanic, five percent black, and five percent white, and it doesn't have room for all of the kids who want to attend. This is one of the few Christian schools in all of New York City. "What a mission field!" Whitaker exclaims. "Millions and millions of people!" Whitaker has 252 of those millions under his wing.

One of those 252 was Sandy, a dark-eyed beauty who had become so rebellious in recent weeks that she wasn't even talking to her teachers. When told she must submit to a paddling for insubordination, Sandy demanded that her parents transfer her to a public school. Her parents wanted her to stay in the Christian school, sheltered from the real New York City, but she had protested so much that they were wavering.

A dramatic transformation came one night when Sandy sat in her room and penned a seven-page autobiography of her teenage existence. In the letter, Sandy told of having arguments with her parents when they objected to her dating boys who smoked pot. She told of her own experiences with marijuana and cocaine. She told of being spaced-out while in public school. We pick up her letter midway.

Well, soon summer comes, and I mean I want to make the most of it. My friends and I are determined to meet so many cute guys. We're gonna make the pool our hangout.

We go to the pool every day and meet so many older guys, and some tell me I'm the only girl they love and that they want to show me how much they love me. I start wondering why I heard that line from five other guys. Well, who knows. There are guys who do fall in love very fast.

My mother tells me they want to use me, and I tell her she's still old-fashioned. She just doesn't want me to go out with guys. Again I disobey her. Until one day this group of people came to my block, and all the guys and girls started running to the building and hiding behind cars. I just stood there wondering what was going on. All my friends were screaming out, "The Bible People!" I was just dancing and laughing at them.

Each of them had Bibles, and there was this lady who was surrounded with little kids. I was just telling myself that they're gonna brainwash them—but suddenly I wanted to go over there too and listen to what that Bible lady was saying. So I started walking over, and my friend pulled me back and told me to stay away from them, but I still wanted to go.

Then I just pulled away and walked to the Bible lady, and she asked me if I died where would I go. I answered purgatory, and she told me there was no such place—that there was only a heaven and a hell. I never had thought of that. Then I knew I would certainly go to hell. She asked me if I wanted to go to heaven, and I thought to myself what kind of a question is that—I mean who doesn't want to go to heaven?

Well, I understood, and I accepted Jesus Christ as my personal Savior. I felt so good—I mean a big load had been removed from my back. At that time, I thought it was the best thing that had ever happened to me.

Then I went back to public school, and I wanted to do my "own thing" again. You can, but there's a little voice inside of me that's always telling me this or that is wrong and making me feel guilty.

I remembered that the Bible said God won't let a Christian practice sin, and if you do get away with it, God will see that you get punished for it for He loves us so much that He doesn't want to see us sin. God cared so much for me that He made it possible for me to go to the Manhattan Christian Academy. Only God knows how much I hated the school and how much I hated everyone that went there. I wanted to go back to public school, and my parents were going to put me back.

Some people were praying for me, and guess what??? I'm still in the school. I mean—you must get the message. I know I got it. God wants me to learn how to be a young lady and not a young drug pusher. He wants to make something very special out of my life.

Principal Whitaker was exuberant the day I visited. Sandy had handed him the letter just that morning, signaling a breakthrough in the school's ministry toward her. Whitaker excitedly talked about how running a Christian school in New York City offers particular challenges. "Sin is treated so lightly in New York City," he said. He spoke of the scripture that says a sign of society's decline will be when those things that are wrong will be considered right in men's eyes. He drew a parallel to homosexuality growing in public acceptance, adding: "To try to transform scriptural values into these kids' minds when they're constantly being polluted on the streets—what a challenge!"

Religious conservatives have a two-word explanation for the pollution on the streets, the havoc in the homes, the turbulence in the schools. They believe children must be sheltered in the Christian school hothouse because a religion has captured the heart of modern-day America and its schools—the religion of secular humanism.

What is secular humanism?

The term embraces the idea of focusing on man's knowledge rather than on God's revelation; the concept of placing man, not God, at the center of his own universe; the philosophy that morals are man made and flexible depending on the situation, not absolutes grounded in divine authority.

Fundamentalists consider secular humanism to be a religion whose purpose is to eliminate belief in God from the arena of public discourse and institutional life. In fact, they cite a U.S. Supreme Court footnote as evidence of secular humanism being a religion. In a 1961 case, *Torcaso v. Watkins,* the Court listed secular humanism as a religion comparable to one of the nontheistic religions such as Buddhism.[3]

To fundamentalists, humanism has become an all-purpose buzzword to explain almost every ill in American life. They believe secular humanists have brainwashed the nation by infiltrating public education, business, government, the news media, labor unions, and even liberal churches. Secular humanism is viewed by fundamentalists as a simple, logical explanation for why everything in American society seems to them to be out of control—why abortion is legal, why divorce is increasing, why homosexuality is accepted, why the traditional family unit is disappearing, and why religious symbols are being deleted from public life.

"Secular humanism in the public schools teaches there are no absolutes," chapel speaker John Caltagirone was telling students at Lynchburg Christian Academy on the day I visited. "God calls it murder; we call it abortion. God calls it drunkenness; we call it alcoholism. God calls it perversion; we call it pornography." Caltagirone told the Virginia students they were indeed lucky to be attending a Christian school where they learn right from wrong.

The Religious Right blames secular humanism for the changes occurring in society and in education. "The secular humanists who control American education—in fact, much of society—are just as religious as you and me. They are driven by a missionary obsession to secularize the next generation," declared Tim LaHaye. "Our public schools have become conduits to the minds of our youth, training them to be anti-God, anti-moral, anti-family, anti-free enterprise and anti-American."

If public schools are that influential and if secular humanists are in control, why don't Christians stay within the public schools and try to wrest control? LaHaye answers: "Because that process would take between ten

---

[3]Torcaso v. Watkins, 367 U.S. 488 (1961), footnote 11 at 495 states: "Among religions in this country which do not teach what would generally be considered a belief in the existence of God are Buddhism, Taoism, Ethical Culture, Secular Humanism, and others." For discussion, see John W. Whitehead and John Conlan, "The Establishment of the Religion of Secular Humanism and Its First Amendment Implications," *Texas Tech Law Review* (Winter 1978): 1-66. In addition, in U.S. v. Seeger, 380 U.S. 163 (1965), the Supreme Court held that even though a person may be an atheist in the ordinary meaning of the term, a belief held by that person may be considered religious, and thus constitutionally protected, if it occupies a place in the life of its possessor parallel to that filled by the orthodox belief in God.

and twenty years. We Christians are not willing to turn our backs on the present generation.''

Martin Marty, an eminent church historian at the University of Chicago, contends the Religious Right created secular humanism so it would have something to attack. ''Whenever you wish to organize a group in America, as diverse and pluralistic as we are, you have to focus on a bogeyman,'' Marty said. ''If you have a diffuse enemy, there is no way to hold a group together and motivate it. When the Christian Right organized—remember that its outlook tends to be Manichean, a simple world where it's God versus Satan, Christ versus the antichrist, modern Christians against who?—the enemy turned out to be secular humanism.''[4]

Fundamentalists point out that secular humanists do have the outward signs of a religion. They have an organization. They have a worldview. They even have a bible.

Their organization is the American Humanist Association, founded in 1941. The association, which publishes *The Humanist* magazine, has about 10,000 members nationwide. Their bible is ''Humanist Manifesto I'' (1933) and ''Humanist Manifesto II'' (1973), an old and new testament so to speak. John Dewey, the father of progressive public education, was a signer of the first document. Signers of the second document included Harvard psychologist B. F. Skinner, author Isaac Asimov, Soviet scientist Andrei Sakharov, officials of Planned Parenthood and Americans United for Separation of Church and State, and numerous Unitarian ministers and university philosophy professors.

The secular humanist worldview depicts supernatural religion and divine revelation as enemies of the rational process. Their worldview opposes the concept of moral absolutes. These are statements from ''Humanist Manifesto II'':

> As in 1933, humanists still believe that traditional theism, especially faith in the prayer-hearing God, assumed to love and care for persons, to hear and understand their prayers, and to be able to do something about them, is an unproved and outmoded faith. Salvationism, based on mere affirmation, still appears as harmful, diverting people with false hopes of heaven hereafter. Reasonable minds look to other means for survival.

> We find insufficient evidence for belief in the existence of a supernatural; it is either meaningless or irrelevant to the question of the survival

---

[4]Marty's quote is in Wray Herbert's ''Fundamentalism vs. Humanism: Cultural Battle Threatens Humanities,'' *Humanities Report* (September 1981): 6.

and fulfillment of the human race. As non-theists, we begin with humans not God, nature not deity.

We can discover no divine purpose or providence for the human species. While there is much that we do not know, humans are responsible for what we are or will become. No deity will save us; we must save ourselves.[5]

The "Humanist Manifesto II" also states that life does not survive the death of the body, that moral values depend on the situation, that orthodox religions unduly repress sexual freedom, that euthanasia (mercy killing) is a right of the individual, that a world government is needed, and that promises of immortal salvation or fear of eternal damnation are both illusory and harmful.

In 1980, sixty-one prominent scholars and writers issued the "Secular Humanist Declaration" that denounces absolute morality and calls for an emphasis on science and human reasoning. The declaration states, "Men and women are free and are responsible for their own destinies and . . . they cannot look toward some transcendental being for salvation." Paul Kurtz, editor of *The Humanist* and a faculty member at the State University of New York at Buffalo, said he drafted the document to counter "the growth of fundamentalism that is a vociferous critic of secular humanism as a scapegoat."[6]

The type of secular humanism decried by the Religious Right had its beginnings in this country in the mid-1800s. It arose during a time of increased secularization and intellectual ferment aroused by rapid advances in science and technology. More attention was being focused on worldly matters, causing an open skepticism toward traditional religion. The Darwin theory of evolution led to a rejection by many of the biblical interpretation of creation. In many ways, today's secular humanism debate is a continuation of those turn-of-the-century arguments.

The Religious Right is suspicious of any form of humanism that focuses on man's knowledge rather than on God's revelation. Since the public schools cannot base learning on religious standards, fundamentalists have grown increasingly suspicious of the philosophy of life that can be

---

[5]"Humanist Manifesto II," *The Humanist* (September-October 1973): 4-9. A partial list of signers is given.

[6]Russell Chandler, "Humanism Under Heavy Attack from Ministers of New Right," Los Angeles Times News Service, the *Washington Post,* 21 August 1981, 14B.

taught in secularized public schools. As a result, those in the Christian school movement believe in the necessity of sheltering kids from the world.

"You can't put a child in a classroom thirty hours a week and have that child not adopt the philosophy being taught," said Eugene St. Clair of Grace Baptist Church School in Portland, Maine. "Many Christians are totally ignorant of humanism being taught in the public schools."

Adds Oklahoma's Michael Pennington: "A person's philosophy of life will be based on his inflow of information. If it's all the characteristics of a reprobate society, then that is what his life will be like. We don't believe in compromising with the world. Christians should contrast the world." The school handbook at Pennington's McCurtain Christian Academy informs students in an opening essay that the schools in this nation once supported the Christian faith but no longer do:

> As the tax-supported public school came on the scene, it was still staffed in overwhelming numbers by Christian teachers who communicated the essence of their faith. Significant changes began to appear in the second decade of the 20th century. A new philosophy came on the scene that denied absolute values, supernatural revelation and wisdom of experience. This philosophy has shaped the thinking of the great majority of the school administrators in this country today. It is increasingly evident that the schools of the United States today are not supporting the faith and commitment of Christian homes.

The Christian school movement in this nation primarily began from negatives perceived in America's public schools. Lately, Christian school leaders talk not just in negative terms of why children shouldn't be in public schools but also in positive terms of why children should be in Christian schools. This view is based on their interpretation of the Bible. Of course, the Bible doesn't really speak to the issue of schools per se, since schools as we know them today did not exist in biblical times. Academic learning took place in the home or synagogue, if at all. But in believing that the Bible speaks to all peoples at all times, conservative Christians say the Bible gives the principles that underlie Christian education. Christian school leaders say that God ordained three basic institutions—the family, the church, and the state. They say the Bible clearly mandates parents to educate their children. These are Bible verses often cited:

> Train up a child in the way he should go and when he is old, he will not depart from it.   —Proverbs 22:6
> And thou shalt love the Lord thy God with all thine heart, and with all thy soul, and with all thy might. And these words, which I command thee

this day, shall be in thine heart: And thou shall teach them diligently unto thy children.   —Deuteronomy 6:5-7a

And, ye fathers, provoke not your children to wrath: but bring them up in the nurture and admonition of the Lord.   —Ephesians 6:4

These schools are considered a Monday-through-Friday continuation of the biblical imperative to "train up a child in the way he should go." Christian schools teach that nowhere in the Bible is the state given a role to play in education. That role, they say, belongs to the home. A Christian school is viewed as an extension of the Christian home. Of course, until recently, the public schools also had been viewed as an extension of the Christian home. But the secularization of the public schools changed that perception, and Christian schools replaced the public schools as this familial extension. Students repeatedly are told that going to a Christian school is not a right but a privilege. School literature emphasizing the positive reasons for Christian education abound.

"There is an important difference between the Christian and the non-Christian viewpoints on a given subject," states a brochure from the Delaware County Christian School in Newtown Square, Pennsylvania. "Even though knowledge is factually the same for both, no subject can be taught in the totality of its truth if the Creator is ignored or denied."

The Whittier, California, Christian High School handbook uses a gardening illustration: "It's the purpose of a Christian school to do more than provide an academic education. We seek to plant, water, and cultivate the seed of faith in Jesus Christ. Our students should graduate first as mature men and women of God and second as academicians."

Dr. A. C. Janney, president of the American Association of Christian Schools, based in Virginia, offers these positives of a Christian education in a pamphlet given to inquiring parents:

> First of all, a good Christian education is going to give your children an academic education. But they're going to get more than that. They're going to learn character based on the lives of those great men of the Bible, and they're going to learn morality and honesty. Christian education will instill in them integrity and responsibility. They're going to learn to be good citizens and good husbands and wives because they will be learning from the Word of God. But it's not just a glorified Sunday school. Day after day, in session after session their teachers, Christian men and women, will vitally affect their lives in a substantial way.[7]

---

[7]A. C. Janney, "Christian Education Doesn't Cost; It Pays" (undated brochure published by the American Association of Christian Schools) 1.

Janney writes that a Christian education doesn't cost; it pays. ''You can't afford not to have it,'' he said. ''It may be that sending your children to a Christian school is cheaper than lawyer's fees to get him out of jail, or sending him to a Christian school and teaching him how to live might be cheaper than raising his children from his broken home.''[8]

Whether it is escapism from the perceived negatives of the public schools or attraction toward the perceived positives of Christian schooling, the fact is that thousands of parents have decided in recent years that the well-being of their children requires a sheltering from the world and a separation from the secularized public schools.

---

[8]Ibid., 2.

3

CLEAN BATHROOMS AND PURE MINDS

Principal Dennis Goodman welcomed a nervous couple and their eleven-year-old son to his office. The boy, a constant disciplinary problem, attended a public school. The parents wanted to enroll him in Goodman's American Heritage Christian School in Yuma, Arizona.

After just a few minutes in his office, Goodman asked the eleven-year-old to step outside and close the door. The boy did so. Goodman then told the parents they needed to stop letting the boy run over them. The embarrassed parents glanced at each other, and the father finally said, "How did you know?"

Goodman accepted the boy as a student. "The first time I talked to him, he put his fingers in his ears. He had a history of doing that, and the psychologists didn't know what to do," the principal said. "Well, I knew what to do. I reached across the desk, yanked his fingers out of his ears, and told him he was going to listen to me. He was shocked, but he listened. I told him if he ever did that again, he was out." The principal paused for dramatic effect. "He's still here."

The parents are pleased, Goodman said, because the boy's behavior is improving and he's learning. Meanwhile, both parents have been converted.

What seems to enhance Christian schools for parents is not just the academic content or the religious flavor, but the entire milieu in which discipline and traditional values are stressed. Just as important as the four R's to many parents is the belief that their children will graduate as responsible, drug-free, well-behaved young people who can get a good job or get into a good college. As a Christian school administrator in Texas noted: "To be successful in college, advanced calculus isn't as critical as teaching perseverance and reading skills and not doing drugs in order to finish your report on time."

The following are among the concepts stressed by Christian schools.

Honesty. Student lockers don't have locks on them at Pensacola Christian School in Florida. "Stealing is wrong. It's a sin. God condemns it. We tell the student if he is caught stealing, he will be expelled," a school official said. There have been three expulsions in a dozen years.

Punctuality. Michael Pennington stands at the doorway, holding a stopwatch, after ringing a bell to mark the end of recess at his Christian school in Oklahoma. The students have ninety seconds to be inside and seated. Pennington says ninety seconds is plenty of time to get a drink of water or run to the bathroom, but not enough time for the boys to think they can keep shooting basketballs indefinitely. "We teach the children that time is important," he said.

Cleanliness. On the first day of school, a male teacher gives a lesson in bathroom etiquette to the boys who attend Grace Heritage School in Research Triangle Park, North Carolina. A female teacher does the same for the girls. "We show them how to lower the seat, how to change the toilet roll paper, how to clean up," the school principal said. "I know it may sound sort of wild. But it was the best day we ever invested. Mr. Parsons, you can come here any time and sit on our seats with confidence."

Truthfulness. At the Southern Baptist Educational Complex in Memphis, "character quality report cards" are sent home to parents along with the regular report card. At the beginning of each grading period, students designate two areas—such as neatness, diligence, humility, punctuality—in which they need to improve. At the end of the grading period, the teacher and the parents mark whether they observed an improvement in the areas. Some students take it seriously; some don't. Recently, a fourth grade girl marked "truthfulness" as a problem area. The puzzled teacher asked her about it since the ten-year-old always had been truthful with her. "The girl started crying and told the teacher she had been taking things from places without paying for them," the principal said. "Because we discovered that flaw in this way, the girl took the things back."

Respect for adults. At some schools, students from kindergarten through twelfth grade jump to their feet when any adult enters the room. The first time this happened to me was in North Carolina. As I stepped inside a ninth-grade history class, the dozen or so teenagers in the room immediately rose and stood military-style beside their desks until the teacher told them they could be seated. This is to show respect for the presence of an adult.

Respect for property. A New York City teenager named Emilio was pleased when his mom decided to send him to a Christian school. He said he figured he could get away with anything there since Christians would have to turn the other cheek all of the time. "One day someone marked on the bathroom wall," Emilio said. "I mean, all it was was a little mark on a wall. No big deal. Every school in New York City has graffiti on the walls. But the principal came down hard on all of us, told us there would be no marking on the walls. He meant business." Sure enough, this is one New York City school with clean bathroom walls.

Responsibility. Fifth-grade teacher David Watson has his hands full with Kenneth, a newcomer to Faith Christian Academy in Trenton, New Jersey. Kenneth had been suspended four times from the public schools. "He came to us totally incorrigible, totally rebellious," Watson said. "His mother said she couldn't control him. He distrusted any male, any adult. He felt totally rejected. He never smiled. He hardly talked. We had to think it through very carefully before deciding to take him. We decided he'd never be reached if we didn't try. . . . A couple of weeks ago, he stole ten dollars in lunch money from the cafeteria. He's paying it back one dollar a week out of his allowance. He's making progress. He's assuming some responsibility. We can see a gradual change."

This milieu in which traditional values are stressed often includes two areas with an immediate visual impression—hair standards and dress codes.

Many Christian schools are like military academies when it comes to hair length and clothing styles. When the parents of today's teenagers were teenagers themselves, rules governing appearance proliferated in the public schools. But the era of student riots and student rights rewrote the rulebook, limiting the authority of public schools in such matters. But strict standards remain in existence in fundamentalist schools today.

At an Iowa school, the principal jutted his chin out and told me: "I passed down an edict to some boys last Friday: Get a haircut or don't come back. I think the Bible teaches that men are to have short hair. That's a principle. I'm not ready to die for hair length or a dress code, but that's our preference for distinction from the world."

Hair-length standards are based on 1 Corinthians 11:14-15, which says it is degrading for a man to have long hair but a glory for a woman. Obviously, it requires a lot of interpretation to be as specific as the student handbook at Grace Baptist Church School in Portland, Maine. The school handbook says: "We find God defines hairstyles and what they should represent." The handbook then proceeds to specify even the manner in which a boy's neckline should be trimmed.

Other Christian schools do not treat hair length as gospel. "I look for spiritual intent, not trying to create standards of hair length based on scripture," a California principal remarked. "I object to the fundamentalists taking what I call convictions and making it doctrine."

Moderate Christian schools, and those with a charismatic leaning, smirk at hair-length rules. An Assembly of God church school in Charlotte, North Carolina, allows boys to have hair of any length. Students there joke about their friends at fundamentalist schools who are required to have "whitewalls"—a band of skin showing around the ear with no hair touching either the earlobe or the collar.

Pat Jarvis, principal of the pentecostal Lighthouse Christian Academy in Gulfport, Mississippi, said he doesn't see any relationship between hair length and a boy's performance as a student or as an individual. "When a boy says 'I believe in Jesus Christ and have faith and try to live it, and I like my hair touching my ears,' what do you answer to that? For some schools, the only recourse is to take the potential for the question away." Principal Jarvis's sandy hair covers his ears and cascades onto his collar. He would have been promptly dispatched to a barber shop had he been a student at a fundamentalist school.

A Christian school in Indiana has a drawing of Jesus on the wall in its twelfth-grade English room. But a boy in this school would be expelled if he had hair that long or wore a beard as Jesus did. Dublin Christian Academy in New Hampshire even prohibits its alumni from returning to campus unless they abide by the strict hair code that bans all facial hair.

Why this captivation with hair length? Why the strict rules, the un-bending insistence, the adamant belief that a boy must have his hair off the collar, off the forehead, off the ears?

It's because fundamentalists consider hair length a symbol. Long hair is prohibited in many Christian schools not because of what it is, but for what it represents. During the 1960s and 1970s, long hair represented re-bellion against authority. The Army shaved the heads of soldiers heading for Vietnam. Youths opposed to the war let their hair grow. Although times have changed, long hair will always signify to many adults a rebellious spirit. Fundamentalist schools won't tolerate a rebellious spirit, so they don't want any outward symbols of it.

The same philosophy applies to dress codes. Many Christian schools, especially those in the A.C.E. camp, require uniforms. The rest allow a diversity of clothing within strict guidelines. Boys wear neat slacks and tucked-in shirts. Shorts, jeans, and tank-tops are taboo at almost all Chris-tian schools.

"The Bible teaches us to be modest in our apparel. That's a distinction between us and the world," said pastor Philip Snow of Idabel, Oklahoma, who himself wears a basic A.C.E. adult uniform—a dark blue suit, a white shirt, a red vest and a red-white-and-blue tie adorned with tiny American flags.

Uniforms are growing in popularity because of the belief that they psy-chologically help students take their work more seriously and socially help to equalize the students, preventing a fashion display by the wealthy and a self-consciousness within the poorly dressed. Snow says families in his church school are not wealthy and most of them sew their children's uni-forms rather than purchase them through A.C.E. A Mississippi principal whose school also is A.C.E. loves the curriculum, but hates the push for conformity. "Sometimes I think the A.C.E. program is trying to turn out automatons," he complained.

But an Illinois principal says the complaining should be directed to-ward the public schools. "If you have a girl who is a modest girl, boy I'll tell you, if she decides to wear a dress to a public school, she'll be laughed at. They wear a uniform to public schools today. It's called bluejeans. There's a total lack of toleration in the public schools."

At all but a few Christian schools, girls are required to wear dresses. Skirts with slits, spaghetti-straps, and tight blouses are out. The dress code for girls is based in 1 Timothy 2:9-10, which tells women to dress mod-estly and says they should be noticed for being kind and good rather than for the way they fix their hair or dress.

The student handbook at the school in Portland, Maine, states: "In 1 Timothy 2:9-10, we find what is pleasing to God concerning women and dress. Our young ladies must wear dresses at all times unless otherwise specified for a gym activity. Dresses are to be knee-length or below. No slits above the knee in skirts and dresses." The handbook says if a student is sent home for unacceptable dress, it will be an unexcused absence. And in the event that a parent is unable to transport the child home for a change of clothing, the handbook states: "The student will be sent home in a taxi at the parent's expense."

At more liberal Christian schools, especially those on the West Coast, the dress code is designed only to prevent extremes. Students have the California look—bronzed skin, blond hair, the guys in tight jeans and the girls in heavy makeup and heels. At Whittier Christian High, a school official said, "We don't believe it's a sin for girls to wear pants."

The Living Word Christian School in St. Charles, Missouri, is a school that once had rules but now teaches concepts instead. The school has students in kindergarten through fourth grade. "One year," pastor Art Reed said, "we required girls to wear dresses. We found out that little girls didn't know how to wear dresses. They'd get on the floor and sit with their panties showing. We realized we didn't need the rule; we needed to teach them mannerisms, teach them what it means to be female. Our objectives are modesty, cleanliness, orderliness. But we don't do it in a legalistic way with a bunch of rules."

Then, beyond the visuals of hair length and modest clothing, there are the personal lifestyle habits taught in these schools. Social drinking and profanity are unacceptable within the fundamentalist Christian community. Lifestyle benefits are tied to scriptural interpretation of such verses as 1 Corinthians 6:19-20, which says a person's body is the temple of the Holy Spirit and the body should be used at all times to glorify God.

Today's strict frown on tobacco has developed only in the past couple of decades. Unlike many public high schools that provide smoking areas for students, even the liberal Christian schools take a hard line on this. Officials at Grand Rapids Christian High in Michigan, especially worried about the number of girls smoking on the sly, instituted a $5 first-time fine for anyone caught smoking on campus. All proceeds go to the American Cancer Society. The first year, the school donated $210. The next year, the fund collected a mere $15. Of course, fundamentalists wouldn't place a monetary pricetag on such an infraction. A student would get one warning, then be kicked out of school.

Another lifestyle belief concerns the influence of the media on today's youth. In Florida, a little girl came home from her Christian school one day and heard the radio playing. She asked her mother if that was rock music, and the mother said yes. "That's sinful," the little girl said matter-of-factly. The mother was incensed and wanted to know who told her that. "My teacher at school," the little girl said. The mother said she would withdraw her girl from the Christian school if anything like that happened again.

At another Christian school in Florida, the administration announced it would discipline any student who went to see Michael Jackson's rock concerts in the Orange Bowl. Officials at Dade Christian School in Miami sent a letter to parents advising them that "rock music is associated with dancing, drinking, the drug scene, and other unacceptable behavior." The note forbade the 1,300 pupils from kindergarten through twelfth grade from attending the Jackson's Victory Tour concerts in 1984. "We are a Christian school. We have rules and regulations," said Michael Nichols, elementary principal of Dade Christian School. "If students want to come here, they voluntarily agree to our rules."[1]

In addition, fundamentalists have a deep skepticism toward television programming and advertising. Here, A.C.E. President Donald R. Howard, referring to the secular world as Egypt, sternly warns against the impact of television:

> Children sit night after night and make heroes out of villains, and idolize every kind of Egyptian pervert, when they should be idolizing the pastor, the Christian teacher, and the Christian principal. Kids think that some of the Egyptian creeps are the greatest things this side of Heaven, and the truth is they are the sorriest things that ever crawled out from under a rock. They are bent on the destruction of the home, the Christian school, the Bible, the family, and everything that you stand for in your Christian school. The whole Egyptian system is as rotten as the Hell that spawned it, and we are ignorant about that thing and are losing our children![2]

Howard tells of the time his parents gave him a TV set at Christmas because they thought his children were missing out on so much. The TV stayed off until the day of the Super Bowl. Suddenly, Howard was tempted since his hometown Dallas Cowboys were playing.

---

[1]"School Kids Told 'No Jacksons Allowed'," *Knoxville News-Sentinel*, 27 October 1984, 2.

[2]Donald R. Howard, *Rebirth of Our Nation* (Lewisville TX: Accelerated Christian Education, Inc., 1979) 244.

"Boy," I thought, "football in the living room." I hurried home to get in on the third quarter. I was fumbling around and got the picture adjusted. "Oh boy! Look at the football game right in the living room; isn't this great? You can sit back and relax and enjoy Cowboy football."

Then the beer commercial came on. I got a sick feeling. Mrs. Howard scurried the kids on out of the room. There was that nauseating ring through our sanctified home. Oh, it made me sick. I mean in the middle of the third quarter of the Dallas Cowboys' Super Bowl game, I had to turn the switch off.

I got a piece of masonite. I had built a three-sectional couch, so I had some upholstering material left over. I covered the piece of masonite with the upholstering and I got one of those sword and shield emblems. . . . I put it right in the middle of that upholstered masonite, slipped the glass out, and slipped that board down in there and sanctified that Egyptian altar. We have a sanctified TV set![3]

When it comes to personal lifestyle beliefs, the student handbook at Calvary Baptist Christian School in Keokuk, Iowa, deserves individual notice for its far-reaching specificity. A plain lunchpail is required because the school doesn't want any "Star Wars fiction" emblems. Students are forbidden from playing video games. School principal Forrest Walker calls Keokuk "a little Chicago" and says a drug culture is tied to video games. Cruising up and down Main Street is prohibited, too. "Main Street is a terrible word around here," Walker says. "There's one bar after another. There's drug trafficking down there. There are teenagers walking down the street drunk. We had some parents leave the school because they didn't think we should control what students do after school hours. Well, whether students know it or not, they project an image of our school wherever they go. I say, 'What is a Christian looking for on Main Street?' Why does he want to go there?"

One year, Walker caught one of his students on Main Street at night. The boy was suspended, and he later withdrew from the school. I had to ask the principal the obvious: "Mr. Walker, just what were *you* doing on Main Street at night?" He replied: "Now, we don't have a police force. We don't go out spying on them. But rumor had gotten back to me that he was down on Main Street and bragging about it. So I just drove on down there to see."[4]

---

[3]Ibid., 245.

[4]I later took my own drive down Keokuk's Main Street and did, in fact, count seven bars in a three-block span.

This control over a student's life even away from school is based on the concept of *in loco parentis*—Latin for "in place of the parent." The concept has all but disappeared in public education, but it remains viable in fundamentalist schools. Let's look at disciplining as an example of *in loco parentis*. Woe to the public school teacher who paddles without permission.[5] And forget about a public school handling a marijuana infraction as the Christian school in Memphis did—with an open rebuke in front of the student's peers. That would be too embarrassing. But James Munro doesn't see anything wrong with that. The principal of Calvary Baptist Academy in Normal, Illinois, said: "If you use the word of God as your barometer, our society is all goofed up. Our society says it's terrible to embarrass. No. God's word doesn't say it's wrong to embarrass. It says it's wrong to do wrong. Embarrassment is not the ultimate crime. I don't go out of my way to embarrass a child, but sometimes a child needs a good embarrassment."

Christian schools believe a disobedient child needs a good paddling, too. Spanking is viewed not as punishment but as loving restraint. School principal Eugene St. Clair of Portland, Maine, pulled out an inch-thick wooden paddle from his bottom drawer and laid it forcefully on his desk. "A carpenter made me this paddle a couple of years ago. It's effective," St. Clair said, while pulling out a notebook. "Let's see. I've given eight paddlings so far this year. There was one for starting a fight, one for lying to a teacher, one for being a classroom problem, and the rest for excessive misbehavior." He administers what he calls "the board of education" to teenagers as well as children.

A student's attitude toward the paddling also is important. A seventh grader named Leon got in trouble at Manhattan Christian Academy in New York City. Teacher Joe Fletcher recalls: "He said he wasn't going to let us paddle him. We told him he would, or else he was out of school. He didn't want the paddling, but he didn't want to be sent away either. We paddled him, but he left as stubborn as before. We told him he was not only going to submit to the paddling, but he'd do so with the right attitude. He finally did. He's really straightening out now."

Christian schools confront problems; they don't avoid them. Sometimes the confrontation is messy and uncomfortable. One day I was vis-

---

[5]Eight states (Hawaii, Maine, Massachusetts, New Hampshire, New Jersey, New York, Rhode Island, and Vermont) and many urban cities ban corporal punishment in public schools.

iting the Alpha and Omega Christian School in Lilburn, Georgia. School principal William Hipps called a teenager named Rachel into his office. He closed the door, but his voice still could be heard in the large classroom across the hall. Hipps is one of those people who couldn't talk softly if he wanted to.

"Rachel, are you on drugs?" he boomed.

The girl spoke softly. Her reply couldn't be heard.

"Well, your personality sure has changed," Hipps cannoned. "You're not doing your work in school. You haven't said 'hello' to me in two weeks, and I want to know what's the problem."

The teenagers in the classroom where I sat stopped doing their work and started twiddling their pencils, as if to give the impression they were working when actually they were listening intently. But her response still couldn't be heard.

"Is there a problem at home? You're still a little girl, but you're rebellious!"

This time Rachel's voice was audible, and cracking: "That's my problem! That's no one else's problem!"

"Oh, yes, it is!" Hipps replied. "Your burden is my burden. As your fellow Christian, I care about you and love you."

There was about fifteen seconds of silence, then the office door opened and Rachel came back to her work desk, head down and silent. Her classmates didn't say a word, but looked at one another and shrugged their shoulders. At lunchtime, the teenagers ate their sack lunches in small groups. Rachel sat by herself, outside the schoolhouse, her back against the front side of the school, just beneath the fluttering American flag. The principal was going to call her parents that day and talk about the problem.

Finally, Christian schools view their purpose not only as learning centers and disciplinary training grounds, but as evangelistic centers. Classes on the elementary level often have invitations to become "born again." That step of faith for those who grow up in the church often comes around the age of eight or nine, which usually corresponds to the developmental stage when children can start making choices based on their own understanding of right and wrong. As a result, the second, third, and fourth grades are key evangelistic years.

On the secondary level, students are periodically confronted about their relationship with Jesus. This mostly occurs through required Bible classes. "I don't make Bible the hardest course in school," one Bible teacher said. "I don't require a lot of outside work, but I do put a lot of emphasis on memorization." She told her class: "As a teenager, there is probably no greater time in life when sin will be pulling at you. You need to remind yourself, 'I am to be more like Jesus this year than last year.' ''

A junior-high chapel service at Calumet Baptist School in Gary, Indiana, challenged the kids to examine the fruit in their lives. Some kids were fidgety; others pensive; still others quietly listened. Allan Frey, heading for Peru as a missionary, gave the message and said afterward: ''An immediate response from them isn't too evident. But the truths they hear sink in. Even here in a Christian school, it can be hard to make a stand. Junior high kids still go along with the crowd. They respond to peer pressure. They know what's right, but some cheat on a test or won't say grace in the lunchroom. A few of the macho boys will intentionally leave their Bibles in their lockers when coming to chapel.''

This combination of *in loco parentis* and evangelistic fervor causes moments of confrontation in Christian schools at times when there might be none in public schools. As one Christian school principal put it: ''In the public schools, kids swear and get by with it. At Christian schools, you have some of the same type of kids. They're here simply because their parents want them to get a good education where there are standards, where it's safe, where there's no profanity and all that stuff. We have kids who occasionally swear, steal, write graffiti. But we do something about it.''

B

THE CLASSROOMS: MAKING GOD THE TEACHER

The American home in 1900 was a place where children learned to honor their father and their mother, to be courteous and honest in their dealings, to be obedient and submissive to authority, and to distinguish right from wrong in all matters. The father was the head of the house, and the mother was his honored companion and helper. Children were lovingly taught what was expected of them and lovingly punished when they disobeyed.

From a history textbook
published by a Christian textbook company.

4

TEXTBOOKS
BATHED
IN COMMENTARY

An American history textbook writes of Franklin D. Roosevelt: "President Roosevelt himself lacked political convictions and principles. . . . The New Deal lengthened the Depression."[1]

---

[1]*United States History for Christian Schools* (Greenville SC: Bob Jones University Press, 1982) 473.

In a chapter on the environment, a science workbook bluntly says: "Most ecologists do not believe in God as the Creator and Sustainer of the world."[2]

A math book poses this multiplication problem with an evangelistic message: "Ace and his friend went soul-winning on five streets. There were nine houses on each street. To how many houses did they go?"[3]

A literature textbook states: "It is a great tragedy that as talented a man as Mark Twain could never find peace with God instead of fighting Him."[4]

The Christian school movement has progressed beyond the mere establishment of alternative schools. In its drive for separation from all trappings of secular education, the movement now has its own textbooks. These books make no pretense of religious or philosophical neutrality. They are written from a fundamentalist perspective, with every subject bathed in scriptural interpretation and political conservatism.

Nonfundamentalists, of course, do not subscribe to this perspective. As a result, the moderate and liberal Christian schools, like the Catholic schools, often use the same books found in the public schools. But the vast majority of America's Christian schools carry their separation from the public schools that extra step by using only books wedded to their philosophy.

The three largest Christian schoolbook publishers are Accelerated Christian Education in Lewisville, Texas; A Beka Book Publications in Pensacola, Florida; and the Bob Jones University Press in Greenville, South Carolina. These three—A.C.E., Beka, and BJU Press—dominate the market.[5] I visited and toured the publishing headquarters of all three.

A.C.E. is more than a book publisher. It is a total approach to education. When a church buys into the A.C.E. system, the church is provided

---

[2]A.C.E. Science #83, 2nd ed. (Lewisville TX: Accelerated Christian Education, Inc.) 5. I asked A.C.E. vice president Ronald Johnson how the curriculum writers could make such a strong statement about ecologists. He replied: "That's a true statement. To get a degree in ecology, you go to a secular university. Christian colleges don't offer degrees in ecology."

[3]A.C.E. Math #1044, 3rd ed. (Lewisville TX: Accelerated Christian Education, Inc.) 26.

[4]A.C.E. English workbook cited in Kenneth Pierce's "A Case for Moral Absolutes," *Time* (8 June 1981): 55.

[5]Two other substantial publishers of Christian school materials are Alpha Omega Publications in Tempe, Arizona, and CSI Publications in Grand Rapids, Michigan. Alpha Omega provides fundamentalist schools with workbooks similar to those of A.C.E. CSI primarily serves Christian Reformed schools.

consultants, workbooks, materials, training—in short, everything. A.C.E. schools tend to be small, averaging just seventy-five pupils in kindergarten through twelfth grade. These are the "teacherless" schools that today are educating half a million children a year. (Chapter 6 describes these schools in detail.)

Since A.C.E. schools have no teachers, the books are all-important. They are consumable paperback workbooks, roughly 40 pages each. A pupil goes through about sixty workbooks a year. They contain short topical essays interspersed with multiple choice, fill-in-the-blank, matching, and short-answer questions. Students write in pencil so their answers can be erased and corrected. Once completed, the workbook itself could be erased and used a second time if needed.

A syllabus of the subject matter covered in the A.C.E. workbooks looks similar to any public school curriculum. A math book for young children has pupils write from one to 100. A social studies workbook for elementary pupils tells the story of Helen Keller and gives examples of sign language. A science workbook for junior high age is devoted to ecology and the balance of nature. A math workbook for teens emphasizes algebraic formulas.

The syllabus may look the same, but the curriculum is written from a perspective radically different from that of secular textbooks. A.C.E. workbooks contain excerpts from "Pilgrim's Progress" and the Bible. Facts are mixed with commentary. In describing the early communal experiments in Jamestown and Plymouth colonies, a social studies workbook says:

> The failures of these colonial communal ventures should be an object lesson to today's advocates of planned socialist economies. God never sanctioned communism. The early church practiced a limited form of socialism, but it was voluntary, short-lived, and for a specific situation. It was never taught as a doctrine of Christianity. Socialism promotes laziness which is definitely contrary to the Scripture.[6]

A.C.E.'s first edition came out in 1973.[7] It proved to be geared to the below-average child. Students with IQs above 100 were breezing through the material and were bored. As a result, a second edition was hurried off the press the following year. This edition proved to be geared to the above-

---

[6]A.C.E. Social Studies #110, 2nd ed. (Lewisville TX: Accelerated Christian Education, Inc.) 17.

[7]Self-instructional material already published by Steck-Vaughn, McGraw-Hill, and Laidlaw served as the basis for A.C.E.'s first edition.

average child. It was way over the heads of many students. Both editions also were filled with errors. The second edition, still in use in many schools, contains misspellings and poor punctuation. For example, in one book the name of the Indian princess Pocahontas is spelled two ways—both of them wrong.[8] Officials admit they rushed both editions, making speed more important than quality. These officials say the third edition has been developed slowly, starting in the late 1970s, with quality as the constant and speed as the variable. The third edition has a core curriculum designed to be mastered by all and then an optional, expanded curriculum for advanced students. The workbooks in this latest edition are better written, more colorful, and typographically cleaner.

For Christian schools with conventional teacher-led classes, the textbook market is dominated by Beka and BJU Press. Every chapter in every book is written through a biblical filter. The physics unit in Beka's junior high science series begins:

> If, in our thinking, we reduce the physical universe to its simplest form, we can say that it is simply matter in motion, and the universe is a machine. This, of course, is by no means a complete description of physical reality, but it is a convenient way for physicists to view the world. The physical universe is God's machine; He designed it; He created it; and He established the physical laws by which it functions.[9]

Beka started publishing in 1975 and now has a full line of brightly colored, mostly softcover textbooks. More than 330,000 students are using Beka books each year.

BJU Press began publishing textbooks in 1974 but has moved much more methodically than either A.C.E. or Beka. Its English series, for example, goes only through the junior-high grades. What has reached the market, however, is highly regarded within Christian school circles. Teachers particularly give high marks to the BJU Press's high-school series in science and history. As Mark Metzger, administrator at Whittier Christian School in California, said: "On the West Coast, Bob Jones has the reputation of being a hard-nosed, legalistic, dogmatic school. But that dogma doesn't show through in their books."

---

[8]A.C.E. Social Studies #110, 2nd ed. (Lewisville TX: Accelerated Christian Education, Inc.). On page 9, the name is spelled "Pocohantas" and on page 10 "Pocohontas."

[9]*Science: Matter & Motion* (Pensacola FL: A Beka Book Publications, 1981) 173. The name "Beka" has intrigued people through the years. "Beka" is the nickname of Rebecca Hall Horton, wife of Dr. Arlin R. Horton, founder and president of Pensacola Christian College and the originator of the textbook curriculum.

The fundamentalist perspective, though, does show through. A sixth-grade math book by BJU Press gives students a budget plan:

> Many families make a budget as they arrange their finances. Most Christian financial advisors suggest that a person or family plan to give the first 10 percent of their income to the Lord and then put the next 10 percent into savings. The amount of money spent on housing should not be more than 30 percent of the total income.[10]

The book gives two illustrations of family budgets. The Johnson family allocates twelve percent of their gross income for tithes and offerings and the Gregory family allocates fourteen percent.

In the quest to rid classrooms of all secular influence, BJU Press has even placed a "Christian student dictionary" on the market. The 816-page dictionary is finely illustrated in brilliant colors, and it contains more than 1,400 photographs and illustrations. To augment definitions, scripture references are added in the margins. You might think that a children's dictionary in a school classroom would be as harmless as, say, a nursery rhyme. But fundamentalists say today's popular student dictionaries with the big print, colorful drawings, and simple definitions are helping transform a generation of children into skeptics and secular humanists.

The publisher of *The Christian Student Dictionary* says a common public misconception is that dictionaries are neutral since they merely define works. But the publisher says: "Dictionaries deal with words and ideas. As a result, any dictionary will reflect the bias of its editorial staff. This is evident in the choice of entry words, in the 'slant' of the definitions, and in the content of the sentences chosen as examples. If the editorial staff has a worldly, godless perspective, so will their dictionary."[11]

BJU Press states in its promotional literature that the four-syllable word "resurrection" is omitted from two popular student dictionaries but the six-syllable word "revolutionary" appears in them all, and that all of the popular student dictionaries include the word "communism" while only half include "capitalism." Besides, BJU Press says the popular student dictionaries define communism "in a neutral or positive way [by] presenting

---

[10]*Math for Christian Schools/6* (Greenville SC: BJU Press, 1981) 220.

[11]A promotional brochure, p. 2, for *The Christian Student Dictionary* (Greenville SC: BJU Press, 1982). The brochure says the selection of words for inclusion in the dictionary was based on citation files, textbook glossaries, and other research materials. Final selection was determined through a comparison of this list with Houghton-Mifflin's word-frequency book and other publications.

just the theory and not the reality of the communist system.''[12] Here is the definition of communism in *The Christian Student Dictionary:*

> A social system in which there are no social classes and little or no private property. The governments of some countries, such as Russia, are based on this idea. These countries actually have a small privileged and powerful ruling class and very little freedom for everyone else.

BJU Press officials say ''Christ'' is omitted from one student dictionary and the others generally describe Him as ''the founder of the Christian religion.'' *The Christian Student Dictionary* gives this definition:

> Jesus Christ, the Son of God; the Saviour of all who trust in Him; the Messiah: ''Christ died for our sins according to the scriptures . . . was buried, and . . . rose again.''

The preface to *The Christian Student Dictionary* says a survey of the leading student dictionaries revealed that not one could be wholeheartedly recommended for Christian young people because many key definitions reflect a skeptical or humanistic bias about the existence of God and about the important doctrines of the Christian faith. In addition, sentence illustrations are said to give examples of dishonesty, disrespect for authority, disregard for Sunday as the Lord's Day, role reversal in home, and the occult.

''Some people wonder about the need for a Christian dictionary,'' John L. Cross, marketing director for BJU Press, told me. ''But our current dictionaries are written by liberals. It shows up in word selections and in role reversals given in the examples, like the woman going off to work and the man staying home with the children.''

For instance, the definition of ''reverend'' in the *Webster's Elementary Dictionary* ends with these examples in parentheses: ''the Reverend John Doe'' and ''the Reverend Jane Doe.'' This would be objectionable to fundamentalists, who do not believe in women serving as pastors. *Webster's* defines ''worship'' as ''deep respect toward God, a god, or a sacred object.'' *The Christian Student Dictionary* defines it as ''the love and devotion of a believer toward God as He is revealed in His Word, the Bible.'' *Webster's* definition is the appropriate one in a generic sense, whereas *The Christian Student Dictionary* defines the word strictly in a Christian sense.

Of course, *The Christian Student Dictionary* is open to the same type of scrutiny it gives secular children's dictionaries. For instance, the word

---

[12]Ibid., 4.

"astrology" is defined as "a false belief that the stars can be used to tell what the future will be." Note use of the word "false." No one suggests that this children's dictionary is word-neutral. It's not meant to be.

The word "conservative" is defined as being "in favor of traditional values and stability rather than abrupt change." The word "liberal" is defined first as "giving freely; generous" and then as "wanting or supporting political or social change." A final definition, with "liberal" capitalized, reads: "One who does not believe that the Bible is the inspired Word of God and therefore does not believe the fundamentals of the Christian faith."

Critics—some within the Christian school movement—say that Christian publishers go overboard in trying to instill their personal political beliefs in children. For instance, Christian textbooks are teaching a generation of children that the United Nations is a complete failure. This is how a Beka history book puts it:

> The United Nations has failed in its dream of ending wars. Since its charter was signed, over seventy-five wars have been fought around the world. Over one billion people have become slaves under Communism, and more than forty million people have been executed by the Communists. The United Nations has not been able to preserve the rights of these people.[13]

The American history textbook published by BJU Press editorializes:

> In spite of the good intentions of many of its supporters, the U.N. has not fulfilled the aspirations of its founders. . . . Its aim of eventual one-world government goes directly against the plan of God, who dispersed the nations at the tower of Babel when they sought to unify. . . . It is not surprising that the U.N. has been unable to accomplish its goals or even to act effectively as a mediator in international disputes. It is a clear illustration of man's failure.[14]

An A.C.E. social studies workbook tells high schoolers that the United Nations was founded as "the last best hope for peace," yet there has been no peace in the world since its establishment. Concerning the U.N. vote to seat Communist China in place of Taiwan, A.C.E. tells students:

---

[13]*New World History and Geography in Christian Perspective* (Pensacola FL: A Beka Book Publications, 1982) 330.

[14]*United States History for Christian Schools* (Greenville SC: BJU Press, 1982) 543.

The vote was met with wild applause and dancing in the aisles—especially on the part of the African representatives. On that day, the U.N. looked like anything *but* an august body of world leaders.[15]

Literature used in Christian schools ranges from the essays of Ralph Waldo Emerson and Henry David Thoreau to the sermons of Dwight L. Moody and Billy Sunday. Modern writers include Ernest Hemingway, Alexander Solzhenitsyn, and Pearl Buck. No essay or short story is presented without comment. The Thoreau introduction in a Beka literature book says:

> Thoreau advocated the same kind of anarchy that characterized the biblical period of the Judges in which every man did what was right in his own eyes. The political views which he expressed in ''Civil Disobedience'' became popular a hundred years after his death, and they have led to much disorder, violence, and anarchy in the name of peace, rights, and individualism.[16]

In introducing the modern fiction writers, Beka says:

> Sherwood Anderson and Sinclair Lewis, who were considered to be Realists, delighted in pointing out what they described as the dullness and hypocrisy of small-town life. They were, in fact, showing their rebellion against the traditional morality and values which were held by the majority of people in the Midwest. Sinclair Lewis's novels *Main Street, Babbit,* and *Elmer Gantry* present an unrealistic view of Christianity and religion in general.[17]

Christian school textbooks point out that some of the more pessimistic writers had unhappy endings—Hemingway committing suicide and F. Scott Fitzgerald drinking himself to death at the age of forty-four.[18]

The distinctiveness of Christian school textbooks is noticeable, to be sure, in literature and science. But the distinctiveness is most prominent in the area of history. For sixth graders, Beka has published *New World History and Geography in Christian Perspective.* The textbook is easy to

---

[15]A.C.E. Social Studies #107, 2nd ed. (Lewisville TX: Accelerated Christian Education, Inc.) 22.

[16]*The Literature of the American People,* vol. 4 (Pensacola FL: A Beka Book Publications, 1983) 101.

[17]Ibid., 367.

[18]Actually, Fitzgerald died of a heart attack and was not a heavy drinker at the time of his death, although he was an alcoholic.

read and packed with color photographs. But even taking into account the age of its target audience, the book takes a surprisingly simplistic view of other cultures. The authors, in fact, make broadly negative generalizations about other cultures. Of the Eskimos, the authors write:

> The governments have started to do for the Eskimos many things the Eskimos used to do for themselves. This has caused laziness and discontent among the Eskimos.

Of the Canadian Indians, the authors say:

> Because they were removed from Christian influences and their tribal customs, many had a hard time adjusting to modern living. Drinking and law-breaking became a problem. They lost their traditional traits of self-reliance because they now expected the government to do for them the things that they should do for themselves.

Of Costa Rica, the authors write:

> People do not work hard, because they know the government will take care of them no matter what they do. The prices for goods have to go up to make up for the time and money wasted by lazy workers.

Of Cuba, the authors state:

> The young people especially have never learned the habit of honest work. They have been provided with schooling, clothing, medical care; they see no need to work for anything. Some young people have become so bored with this lazy life that they have committed suicide. Others have turned to alcohol, drugs, or robbery.

In addition, Beka's history text reveals the musical inclinations of various peoples: "The Eskimos love to sing, and one of their favorites is 'What A Friend We Have in Jesus' sung in the Eskimo language," and "They (the Canadian Indians) became expert hymn singers, their favorite song being 'Nearer, My God, To Thee.' "[19]

The story of young George Washington and the cherry tree is told as true, with a fatherly lecture embellishing it:

> George followed his father into the woodshed. Using a small birch rod, Mr. Washington gave George a sound whipping. As soon as the last stroke

---

[19]*New World History and Geography in Christian Perspective* (Pensacola FL: A Beka Book Publications, 1982) Eskimos, 37; Canadian Indians, 46; Costa Rica, 141; and Cuba, 337.

was finished, Mr. Washington held his whimpering son in his big, strong arms and gently said, "It is over now, son. I commend you for your honesty. I will now try to forget this, but do not let yourself ever forget the damage that can be done when you do not control your temper."[20]

Then, in describing life in the United States at the start of the twentieth century, Beka provides this idyllic account:

> The American home in 1900 was a place where children learned to honor their father and their mother, to be courteous and honest in their dealings, to be obedient and submissive to authority, and to distinguish right from wrong in all matters. The father was the head of the house, and the mother was his honored companion and helper. Children were lovingly taught what was expected of them and lovingly punished when they disobeyed.[21]

This account of American life at the turn of the century recalls Will Rogers's famous quip: "The schools aren't as good as they used to be, but they never were." If secular textbooks distort history in one direction, as is frequently charged, Christian textbooks must beware not to equally distort it in the other direction.

From the Mayflower Compact to the modern era, Christian school textbooks portray the United States as a nation blessed by God in its establishment but now facing God's judgment because of sin. To fundamentalists, *history* is actually *His Story*.

The opening sentence in BJU's American history textbook for high school students is: "The cross of Christ is the focal point of human history." The book is built upon that rock. So, keeping that statement in mind, let's journey through America's history via this BJU high school history text.[22]

Christopher Columbus:
Whether he was a true Christian or only a devout Catholic, . . . Columbus believed that his decision to sail west resulted from God's leading.

---

[20]Ibid., 226.

[21]Ibid., 303.

[22]*United States History for Christian Schools* (Greenville SC: BJU Press, 1982) Cross of Christ, 15; Columbus, 26; Founding Fathers, 86; French and Indian War, 104; George Washington, 179; Great Revival, 197; Slavery, 237; Confederate revivals, 301; Civil War aftermath, 323; Labor union strikes, 332; Compulsory education, 335; Woman suffrage, 436; World War II, 515; Joseph McCarthy, 549-50; Lyndon Johnson, 571; Cultural Revolution, 575; Vietnam, 577; and the Middle East, 577.

Our Founding Fathers:
Those who founded the American colonies were, for the most part, deeply religious. Not all of them were Christians in the biblical sense of the term, but they all recognized God as the Creator and Ruler of the earth. . . . It is no accident that this nation eventually became the strongest and most prosperous on earth.

French and Indian War:
Perhaps the most significant result of the war was that it determined that America would be a Protestant nation that would offer both religious and civil liberty to its people. . . . If France had won, it seems fairly certain that America would have become a Catholic nation and would, of necessity, have been forced to live under the combined absolutism of church and state.

George Washington:
At his inauguration, Washington established several precedents that show his respect for God. When he took his oath of office, he placed his hand on the Bible, as all presidents since have done. At the end of the oath he added the words ''so help me God.'' With these four short words he indicated the immensity of his office and his need for God's help in executing its duties.

The Great Revival:
To credit the survival of the fledgling republic wholly to the Constitution and political leadership is hardly realistic. Indeed, many Christians believed that America would have died in its early decades, despite its Constitution and its statesmen, had it not been for another very important influence. Just when it was most needed, a great revival resurrected the national morality.

Slavery:
The story of slavery in America is an excellent example of the far-reaching consequences of sin. . . . It resulted in untold suffering—most obviously in the black race, but in the white as well. It led, at least in part, to the division of a nation and a bloody war to reunite it. It has instilled a tension and even a bitterness, in some cases, between the races in the United States.

Confederate revivals:
Throughout the Civil War there were continuing revivals in the Confederate army. . . . Because of the influence of Lee, Jackson, and other Christian officers, many Confederate soldiers were converted. Numerous Bible-preaching churches were then established in the South following the war, and to this day the Old South is referred to as the ''Bible Belt.''

Civil War aftermath:
These were not pleasant years for the United States. Hatred and selfishness had led to a war that nearly destroyed the nation. . . . Many nations have disintegrated under less trying conditions. Yet God graciously preserved

this nation, through no merit of its own, for His own reasons.

Labor union strikes:
Strikes are not immoral in themselves. Workers should be free to quit work, even to quit work en masse, if they wish. Strikes become immoral, however, when workers destroy property, or when they use force or intimidation, such as picket lines, to prevent others from working or taking the strikers' jobs. Most of the major labor strikes in our history have been immoral.

Compulsory education:
Though it was noble to provide education for those who wanted it but could not afford it, the advent of public schools presented certain dangers. It removed the control of the child's education from the parents and placed it with the state governments. It contributed to the thinking that a free education was a right, rather than a privilege.

Woman suffrage:
Many reformers believed that women could use their vote to abolish corrupt institutions and practices. Ironically, however, the first national election held under the provisions of the Nineteenth Amendment brought to the White House the handsome Warren G. Harding, whose administration was one of the most corrupt in the nation's history.

World War II:
A most important consequence of World War II was the opportunity it provided the Soviet Union for territorial expansion. Despite the fact that the Soviets contributed very little to the outcome of the war—nothing, in fact, to the defeat of Japan—they were the main beneficiaries at the end, receiving, in essence, half a continent for their participation. For this reason the war served to usher in another era—that of the Cold War and the rapid growth of the Communist threat to freedom.

Senator Joseph McCarthy:
Though many of his accusations were indeed true, McCarthy was far too careless with them, thereby injuring or even destroying the reputations of a number of innocent people. . . . The liberal media soon discredited him, and he was censured by the Senate. More care for the truth would undoubtedly have increased his effectiveness; as it was, his behavior did considerable damage to his good cause.

Lyndon B. Johnson:
Few other presidents have known how to work with Congress as well as Johnson. Because he was also politically unscrupulous and unprincipled, he could use his advantages to the utmost.

The 1960s Cultural Revolution:
America was seeing in its youth the product of the godless, materialistic society it had become. Since World War II the public schools had become secular. The theory of evolution had reduced man to the status of a mere

animal. Permissiveness in behavior, including sexual behavior, was encouraged. Duty to God was replaced by duty to society. Without any real reason to maintain high moral and ethical standards, the youth threw off all restraint.

Vietnam:
Limitations placed on U.S. military personnel by their own government, held virtually hostage by a hostile press and the constant threat of riots, made winning the war impossible.

The Middle East:
The Middle East has remained the critical area of the world not only because of its vast oil resources, but also because Israel is the focal point of God's plan for the last days. As the return of Christ draws nearer, the world's attention will be on Palestine.

Finally, this American history textbook characterizes the 1970s and early 1980s as a period of American weakness. The book takes a harsh view of Richard Nixon, saying: "President Nixon, of course, is remembered as a man of weak character—one who sacrificed higher principles for personal power."[23] The book gives a factual account of Watergate and says Nixon was unable to weather the storm because of his "own ineptitude and unrepentant spirit. . . . He looked, spoke, and acted like a criminal." The authors criticized the news media as well:

> Every U.S. president has been fallible. Presidents have broken the law and violated public trust almost innumerable times. By his own definition, Thomas Jefferson exceeded his powers in purchasing Louisiana. Grover Cleveland admitted to fathering an illegitimate child. Dwight Eisenhower acknowledged that he had lied about the U-2. Yet many consider these men exemplary presidents, while viewing Richard Nixon as contemptible. Why the inconsistency?
> Perhaps the most important cause of the unusual outcry over Watergate was the power of the press. Some journalists, eager to "make a story" or to popularize their bylines, pursued the issue relentlessly, always keeping it in the spotlight. The public fell victim to this manipulation, in essense [sic] living at the mercy of the most influential typewriter.[24]

The history book portrays Gerald Ford as a man who, because of the troubled times in which he served, was forced to avoid aggressive leadership. Jimmy Carter is cited as "an example of weak leadership," spe-

---

[23]Ibid., 583.

[24]Ibid., 592.

cifically his handling of the Panama Canal treaties and the Iranian hostage crisis. Ronald Reagan, the textbook says, was elected in a 1980 landslide largely because of the support of the New Right, which represents a renewed conservative and Christian political activism.

The history book concludes with a brief epilogue mourning America's decline and proclaiming the need for restoration. The textbook blames the nation's decline on the splintering of the home, the weakening of the church, and the massive swelling of the government. But the authors offer this challenge to students:

> Rather than merely lamenting the evils of modern America or condemning others for their failures, Christian citizens of the United States should rise to the challenge of restoring their nation—originally a gift from God—to be that nation ''whose God is the Lord.''[25]

These citations are from typical textbooks used in thousands of Christian schools across the land. Of course, these books are considered mere supplemental texts to the ultimate textbook—the Bible. In many schools, pupils keep their personal Bibles on their desks and refer to them often in their work.

Now that textbooks from a Christian perspective are available, school leaders say they now have a full complement of tools to offer an education they describe as truly by-the-Book.

---

[25]Ibid., 609.

5

A DAY
IN THE LIFE
OF LIVING WORD

The little boy took a couple of drib-
bles and, with a shout, heaved the red ball to a playmate. The playmate's
outstretched arms couldn't reach high enough, and the chase was on—the
ball merrily bouncing downhill across the asphalt parking lot and the playmate gamely giving chase.

Beth Uphoff watched the boy finally catch up with the ball and then
she called out: "Line up!" The time was nine o'clock, and it was time to
begin another day at Living Word Christian School in Manhattan, Kansas.

Fifty kids came running, and Miss Uphoff had to remind them once
again to slow down. They subdivided into lines based on age and grew

quiet. "Let's see how straight you can get those lines," Miss Uphoff said cheerily. When satisfied, she gave the go-ahead for the students to enter the building—a former roller rink converted into a charismatic church in 1982. Teachers had reported to work an hour earlier for their daily prayer time. Now, it was the pupils' time to pray. Standing in a circle in their room, the kindergarten pupils prayed aloud in short sentence prayers: "God, thank you for this day" and "Bless our teacher."

The school day at Living Word Christian School doesn't begin with math or phonics or social studies. It begins with prayer and Bible verses. After the prayer time, kindergarten teacher Cecilia Myers called on five-year-old Travis to review the alphabet. He stood, with shoulders straight and hands in pockets, and began:

A—All have sinned and come short of the glory of God. Romans 3:23.

B—Believe on the Lord Jesus Christ, and thou shalt be saved. Acts 16:31.

C—Children, obey your parents in the Lord: for this is right. Ephesians 6:1.

These are the ABCs—the backbone of education—and at Living Word each letter of the alphabet is tied to a scripture verse that begins with that particular letter. The kindergarten children not only learn the alphabet, but they memorize more than two dozen scripture verses in the process. This particular day—12 May 1986—Travis went through the letter R, quoting eighteen Bible verses by memory along the way. By the time the school year ended two weeks later, Travis and three others in the class were able to go through the entire alphabet of Bible verses.

Meanwhile, the junior-high students had put up their backpacks and books and gone into the sanctuary for the Monday morning chapel service. For the next half hour, one of the mothers led the thirteen teenagers in singing songs and choruses. The teachers occasionally raised their hands in praise and said "Amen." At one point, spontaneously, many of the teenagers standing in a semicircle started holding hands while singing. Then they sat and heard a Christian testimony from one of the teachers.

At a few minutes after ten o'clock, the junior-high students returned to their classroom to begin the first academic lesson of the day: independent and dependent clauses.

"Just as you are dependent on your parents, the dependent clause in a sentence is dependent on the subordinating conjunction," Miss Uphoff told the seventh and eighth graders. The class worked sentence exercises in their 1985-revised grammar and composition textbook published by A Beka Book Publications. Students underlined the subjects, put two lines beneath the verbs, put parentheses around the dependent clauses and circled the subordinating conjunctions in each sentence. During the lesson for seventh and eighth graders, the three ninth graders sat at their desks doing other work. Occasionally one of them raised a head and listened to the discussion on clauses, but they were free not to. They had covered that ground the year before.

This is not a one-room schoolhouse of old, with all grades in one room, but it does have similarities. Living Word Christian School has five teachers and fifty pupils in grades K-9. The school is adding one grade a year until it is a twelve-grade school. The half-day kindergarten class has six pupils. The first and second grades are in the same room. So are the third and fourth grades. And the fifth and sixth. Thirteen pupils are junior-high age, and they spend all day in the same room.

Living Word Christian School is not representative of the Christian school movement in this country. No single school is. But as a school externally and as a philosophy-toward-education internally, it typifies why the Christian school movement is mushrooming nationwide.

Manhattan is a city of 35,000 located two hours west of Kansas City. It's the home of Kansas State University. Residents of Manhattan are proud of their public schools and, with few exceptions, praise the quality of public education. Public school students routinely score above national norms on standardized tests. The racial composition of the public schools is eighty-six percent white, seven percent black, five percent Asian and two percent Hispanic.

Yet even in a small community such as Manhattan—away from racial busing and court-ordered integration plans, away from a populace unhappy with its local public schools, away from the Bible Belt—Christian schools are emerging. Manhattan has two of them. Living Word Christian School, which has an eight percent minority enrollment, is operated by an independent charismatic church. Across town, a fundamentalist Baptist congregation sponsors one of the "teacherless" A.C.E. schools with thirty pupils enrolled.

Lest the numerical impact of these Christian schools be exaggerated, the Manhattan public schools have 5,710 students, and the Catholic schools in the city enroll 307 students. These two new Christian schools, with their combined enrollment of 80, represent a mere one and three-tenths percent of the school-age population. But this is eighty students more than were going to Christian schools in this city when the 1980s began, and the Catholic Diocese has announced plans to close its high school because of declining enrollment while Living Word is in the process of adding the high-school grades.

Living Word Christian School is part of a rapidly growing church started in 1981 through home and campus Bible studies. The church met for a time in a public elementary school before moving into the former roller rink in 1982. Church membership grew from fifty to 275 in three years, and pastor Gary Ward says, "We're believing God for a thousand people." Ward himself was a public school teacher for eighteen years before going into the ministry. As a biology teacher at Manhattan High School, Ward said he wrestled with "God's call into the ministry" for two years. "I still did the best I could for my students. Teaching is precious to me," he said. "But my heart was no longer in it." He then accepted the pastorate. "I've never been to Bible school. I've never been to seminary. I was just ordained by the Holy Spirit."

When Ward left teaching, he thought he was leaving education behind. But in his second year as pastor, parents came to him with a suggestion for a Christian school. Ward said he spent three days praying and studying material about Christian schooling before deciding it was the right thing to do. The school started with twenty-eight students, most of them children of church members.

The state of Kansas is highly accommodating toward private schools. The state requires that every school have a license to operate, but all that is required to obtain a license is a health and safety inspection and a pledge that all teachers are competent. Teachers do not have to be state certified, although all but one at Living Word are. The school has not sought state accreditation. The school handbook states: "Living Word Christian School is not interested in using textbooks adopted or approved by the state. Many of those texts are developed by secular authors who reject fundamental Christian principles and therefore are saturated with humanistic values." The handbook tells prospective students that graduating from an accredited school is not necessary to enroll in a college or university since admissions normally are based on student aptitude and achievement as determined through standardized tests.

Unlike the public schools, Living Word Christian School selects its student body. Before enrollment, all students and parents are interviewed by the principal or another official. At the discretion of the school, applicants also may be asked to take an admissions test. School policy states that pupils are "carefully selected in order to maintain a student body of high academic and moral Christian standards."

A strong academic emphasis begins in the kindergarten year. Whereas many public schools consider kindergarten more of a socialization year for children, the A Beka Book curriculum for kindergarten covers topics usually reserved for first or second grades in public schools. At Living Word, not only do the kindergarteners learn the alphabet, but they also learn phonics. On the day I visited, Mrs. Myers was pointing to a phonics chart to help groups of students learn consonant blends. Then the boys and girls, in ability groupings, read from Beka books. Mrs. Myers was the epitome of patience as her young ones learned to read. A five-year-old boy took more than thirty seconds looking at a sentence before finally saying, ''The bird sat on her nest.'' The wait had been worth it. ''Top job!'' Mrs. Myers said. The pupils read the story in round-robin fashion. At the end, everyone got a blue star. Their homework assignment: learn a dozen words such as ''proud'' and ''joy'' from the Beka book.

Mrs. Myers spends the mornings as the kindergarten teacher and the afternoons as principal. As teacher, she operates a highly structured class. Kindergarten students spend almost all of their time in learning situations as opposed to pure play time during their three hours in the classroom each day. To learn spelling, children went to the blackboard two at a time and spelled words as the teacher called them out. The first word was ''spell.'' One boy wrote ''spael'' and the other ''spel.'' Mrs. Myers had them erase the wrong letters or add the appropriate letter to get the word correct. After all of the children had a turn at the blackboard with such words as ''tree'' and ''clap,'' the class next counted in unison to 100 by fives, then by tens. This was followed by a flash-card game of addition. One girl was having a difficult time of it that day, and Mrs. Myers told her softly: ''Pray that God gives you the answer.''

In the first/second grade class, students were working some multiplication and division problems and also learning to write in cursive. Linda Scott gave students the assignment and asked, ''Any questions?'' Matt raised his hand and said: ''Yesterday I opened my mouth and a bug flew in, and it never flew out.'' Teachers get accustomed to ''questions'' such as that, and Mrs. Scott replied without a pause: ''That's good protein.''

Later, a boy came to Mrs. Scott's desk and said that a tooth hurt. Mrs. Scott was sympathetic and asked the boy if his tooth *had* to hurt. The boy said no. ''Can God get rid of the pain?'' Mrs. Scott asked. The boy said yes. She told him he should pray right then about it, and the boy closed his eyes while standing next to the teacher's desk and prayed: ''Please help my tooth not to hurt and help it to feel better.'' The teacher said ''Amen,'' and the boy returned to his chair.

Charismatic churches place more emphasis on healing than do mainline denominations. "Our church is very strong on healing," said Mrs. Myers. She said teachers often pray with children about physical aches and pains. In the case of the boy with the toothache, Mrs. Myers said the boy certainly would be encouraged to see a dentist if the tooth continued to ache. "We believe God can heal, either through doctors or through prayer," she said.

One of the walls of the church sanctuary bears testimony to the healing aspect of the church ministry. Hanging on the wall, beneath the words "Jesus Is My Healer," are a cane, a neck brace, an empty beer bottle, packs of cigarettes, a bottle of pills, and a mist for bronchial asthma—all items that church members said they had been healed from needing.

Lunchtime came at the school, and this meant sack lunches. The church facility has no cafeteria, although a microwave oven is available for the teachers. In the junior high room, five boys were huddled around two chess sets and another boy was reading a Louis L'Amour western while eating sandwiches brought from home. Girls sat eating and talking in small clusters.

At her desk, Miss Uphoff ate a sandwich and acknowledged that she didn't know how the one-room schoolhouse teachers had done it. She said the academic balancing act required in having all seventh, eighth, and ninth graders in a single room all day was frustrating at times but did work.

Later, while on recess duty, she explained why she had become a Christian school teacher. She graduated with a degree in elementary education from Kansas State University in 1981 and taught for several years in a small public school system in Kansas. "I was seeing a real decline in standards there—eighth graders who couldn't read, and I couldn't teach them. At this same time, some people said, 'You're a Christian and you should be in a Christian school.' I never liked the idea. I had such a negative attitude toward Christian schools. It was an escapist trend. I thought that kids wouldn't be able to deal with reality once they got out of the hothouse. I felt like I should be in the public schools, witnessing to them there. But the Lord changed my heart. I saw a vision for Christian education."

Miss Uphoff said she realized that an army doesn't send soldiers to war without first training them. She said Christian children need the same nurturing and training before facing the temptations that society offers. English grammar is English grammar, be it in a public school or at the Living Word Christian School. But Miss Uphoff said the difference between the two educational systems is that Living Word continually reminds students that God has a plan for their lives. "We're not instilling an elitist attitude," she said. "But we do tell them they know right from wrong. We tell them, 'You're going to be the leaders of tomorrow.' We tell them,

'Maybe you'll be president of the United States someday.' School is a place to get them thinking about God's purpose for their lives.''

At recess, I visited with many of the junior high kids. They complained about not having a cafeteria. They complained about having no school sports. They complained that tight scheduling prevented them from having much time to talk with each other during the school day. They complained about having to spend all day in one tiny room rather than getting to move room-to-room each hour as in the public secondary schools. But they merely complained; they weren't embittered. In fact, considering they were junior-high age, they were quite complimentary of Living Word Christian School, and many of them volunteered a lot of positives about the school along the way.

"They care about you here," one said. "Here you get the truth," said another. They were profuse in their praise for the teachers, and many of them indicated they planned to be back next year—and that it was their own decision. Those who didn't plan to return cited sports as a big reason they wanted to be in a public school. "My time here is almost up," one teenage boy said, as if it were a prison sentence. Some of the girls standing nearby laughed. The boy said he was anxious to go to a school with more people, with bigger programs, with sports. But even *he* had a kind word to say: "My time is up, but I'd recommend it for a year or two. I haven't regretted it.''

Back in the classrooms, which all have a photograph of President Reagan on the wall, students do a lot of textbook reading aloud. During the science segment of the day, junior-high students took turns reading one page each from their Beka science chapter on broadcasting. Living Word teachers say the method improves student reading and comprehension skills. A byproduct, of course, is that this method of instruction doesn't require much teacher preparation.

Some lessons sparkle; others fizzle. Chris Poersch, who has three sons attending the school, is a teacher who rotates from room to room giving art and science lessons. In the junior high room, the lesson on broadcasting principles obviously was not her specialty. She tried an experiment to show the concept of radio waves. Tying a jump rope to a door knob, a student gave the rope some whip-like motions. But the rope had some knots in it and never simulated waves. So she went to the blackboard, drew some waves and struggled through an explanation of frequency, wavelength, and amplitude.

But in the third/fourth grade class, Mrs. Poersch's lesson on skin held pupils in rapt attention. The lesson began with pupils sticking their fingers in a bowl of water and holding their hands in front of a fan. They all agreed that their wet fingers were cooled when held in front of a fan. Mrs. Poersch read several paragraphs from an elementary science book about the cooling properties of skin, then provided another illustration. "Many of you are sweating—or perspiring—when you come in from recess," she said. "You like the fan on, and you get in front of it so that the air blows on your skin. Right?" The kids nodded. She said the same cooling principle is at work.

The topic then switched to what happens when the skin is cut. "When Carrie fell down and scraped her shoulder this morning," said Mrs. Poersch, "we put an antiseptic on it to keep the germs out. That's why you wash out a cut and put a Band-Aid on it. God made your body where it can heal." That prompted a second-grade boy to tell about someone he knew who smashed his finger with a hammer and got so mad that he swung the hammer over his head and the claw struck the man in the head and he had to get stitches. The teacher listened to the sentence that never really ended, but kept having more "ands" to piece together new thoughts. When the boy stopped to catch his breath, Mrs. Poersch nodded her head in acknowledgment of the story and turned it into an object lesson by saying, "Anger didn't pay off, did it?"

After some talk about stitches and goosebumps, the lesson gravitated to nerve endings in fingers. "When touching a hot oven, you don't have to think about it. God put inside of you something called a reflex. Your body will move away from pain." The subject soon turned to fingers, and Mrs. Poersch had the pupils look at the folds on their knuckles. "Who made your fingers?" she asked. "God," the students replied. Mrs. Poersch explained that the folds of skin on the knuckles were necessary for a person to be able to bend the fingers. "God knew how to make them bend," she said.

As the final science project of the day, the teacher let students make their own fingerprints with an ink pad. "No one has a pattern like anybody else," she said. One pupil added, "Snowflakes aren't the same either." The teacher agreed with her and pointed out that God not only made every snowflake different but that every person is unique, too.

The academic lesson had dealt with the properties of skin. But the word "God" had been part of the conversation throughout. A merger had occurred between the educational and the religious. This is commonplace, and desired, in Christian schools. This merging of education and religion occurs in other realms of student and teacher life, too. For example:

Discipline. When a child is paddled, prayer follows immediately. Teachers want to make sure the child is repentant of the wrongdoing and not simply angry about getting a paddling. Few paddlings occur, however. Most disciplinary action is handled through a ticket system. When a student gets too many tickets, there is a price to pay—usually a temporary loss of privileges.

Sex education. As Living Word adds the high-school grades, the school will face developing relationships between boys and girls. This year, the faculty offered a one-time session just for boys and another one just for girls on the physical body and on choosing girlfriends and boyfriends. "We teach them it's okay to have these feelings, but you must keep God first," Mrs. Myers said. The student handbook adds:

> The Living Word Christian School provides opportunities for boys and girls to cultivate friendships with the opposite sex. In some instances, these associations will deepen into more than passing friendships. This is both natural and expected. However, all such friendships must be handled in a responsible manner. Public displays of affection, such as holding hands or other physical intimacies, will be considered in poor taste and will not be allowed.

Evolution. "We teach creationism," Mrs. Myers said. "God created man. He didn't create ape to evolve into man. We believe the Bible, not evolution." Pastor Gary Ward—the former high-school biology teacher—said he, too, believes in a literal interpretation of the creation account in Genesis. "As a trained biologist, I hung on to evolution myself for a long time," he said. "In my early years, I taught evolution of human life." Ward said he doesn't reject the concept of evolution itself; he knows that evolution does occur. But he rejects evolution as the method of creation of humankind.

Teacher salaries. All teachers at Living Word get the same paycheck—$1,100 a month. "It's a sacrifice," Beth Uphoff said matter-of-factly. "I'd be making several thousand dollars more if I were still teaching in the public schools." Mrs. Scott also taught at a public school before joining the Living Word faculty. "We look at ourselves as ministers as well as educators," she said. "Salary is a gift of God. I'm not saying I'd do it for free. I do have financial obligations. But God has allowed me to do this, and He picks up the slack."

The school day at Living Word ended at 3:30, and it ended just as it had begun—in the Bible. A fifth-grade girl sat in a chair next to her teacher's desk, quoting Psalm 91 by memory as the teacher followed along in her Bible.

Four weeks later, when school had ended and summer had arrived, Living Word's faculty sponsored an information session for parents within the community who were curious about Christian schooling. Seven families not connected with the church attended.

"Christian schools have literally mushroomed all across this country, but this was not our reason for starting our Christian school," Pastor Ward told the parents who showed up. "Our purpose is to provide a Christ-centered academic education."

Ward said the school serves as an extension of the family, not as an escape from the public schools. "We're not mad at the public schools," he said, adding that public education has many aspects not found at Living Word. "There's a lot we don't have," Ward said. "We don't have a football team. We don't have a marching band. We don't have enough typewriters. We don't have a lunchroom." Without breaking stride, Ward shifted the emphasis. "We don't have a drug problem. We don't have an alcohol problem, or classes that teach about contraceptives. We don't have a lot of things."

Ward said the school, though, does have an emphasis on academic excellence within a spiritual framework. "I guess there are some who think that all that the children do is sit around and pray. We think God's kids ought to be the wisest children—knowing how to use whatever abilities they have to the best." Ward said the school places high expectations on students. "This is a nonanxiety-producing pressure," he said, "showing they can be more than they think they can be."

Mrs. Scott told the parents that Christian schooling meant a lot more work on their part. Without a transportation program, parents must get their children to school and back home each day. Without a lunch program, parents must fix a sack lunch each day. They also must initial their child's homework slips each night to show involvement with the child's learning process. Parents also must commit themselves to participating in school workdays or parent programs on such topics as rock music and the availability of Christian toys.

"It's easier to send your child to a public school," Mrs. Scott said. "Just send them out the door and put them on the bus. But many of our parents say that the drive (to and from the school) can be a time of spiritual feeding and nurturing. It's a time to establish calmness. This can be a high quality time with your child, a time when you get into the heart of your child."

Pastor Ward then brought up the subject of money. "We don't have a tuition," he said, pausing as the parents looked up quizzically. "This is partly inspired by the court system. This isn't a private school operated as a business on the side. It's a ministry of the church."

A handout to parents explained the financial arrangements. The pastor said it costs roughly $160 a month to educate a child. "Living Word Church will pay half that amount, and we ask parents to pay the other half," Ward said. "This is not a tuition, but a donation, and as such it is fully tax deductible for you as a contribution to the ministry of the church."

The cost is not all that unusual for Christian schooling, although few Christian schools are as bold about declaring the payment to be a tax-deductible contribution rather than tuition. Tuition at the schools I visited averaged about $100 a month per child. Some Christian schools were elitist academies with tuitions in the $4,000 a year range. These tended to be the nonfundamentalist and noncharismatic Christian schools. The newer fundamentalist schools appeal primarily to middle- and lower-income families by offering tuitions as low as thirty dollars a month. Students from poor families sometimes mow the grass or sweep floors after school to pay their way. At the Living Word parent orientation session, one mother asked if she could work in exchange for tuition. Ward replied: "If you have more time than money, we'll work with what you have."

The pastor said parents would be expected to contribute eighty dollars a month to the church above any regular tithe. If a family saw that it could not do so, then the family was asked to notify the church office and say how much could be contributed that month. "We'll just speak a blessing to you. We'll stand in agreement with you that God will provide your needs," Ward said. "If God told you to put your child in a Christian school, He will provide a way. . . . It is certainly not our intent to put anyone in financial bondage."

But Ward said parents should be open to creative financing. "Some may have a job where you can work a few hours overtime each month. Others may find ways to supplement your present source of income," stated the financial information sheet given to parents. "A number of women in the Manhattan area clean houses for twenty dollars apiece, spending two or three hours per house. Cleaning only one such house per week would pay for your part of the entire month's education for a child. Ask God what He would have you to do."

At the end of the ninety-minute meeting, most of the families stayed around to see the classrooms, look through Beka books on display, and talk with the teachers and the pastor. The majority of parents took application forms home. Combined with growing church interest and a banner kindergarten roundup, it appeared that Living Word would have its largest enrollment ever the following year.

6

SCHOOLS
THAT HAVE
NO TEACHERS

It is unusually quiet inside the Mc-
Curtain Christian Academy in rural Oklahoma. No teacher's voice booms
out an explanation of nouns and verbs. No teacher's chalk scratches the
blackboard during a multiplication exercise. No teacher's ruler touches a
map in a discussion of European alliances during World War II. In fact,
there are no teachers at all.

This is an Accelerated Christian Education school—one of some 5,000
A.C.E. schools educating half a million children nationwide. Roughly a
third of all Christian schools in the United States operate with the A.C.E.
curriculum.

The concept of no teachers in a school is revolutionary. Students in individual cubicles work silently at their own pace, mastering workbooks that stitch Bible verses into lessons on nouns and verbs, multiplication problems and European history. When baffled, students raise one of the small flags at their study carrels. Each student has a six-inch American flag and Christian flag set. When needing academic help or even permission to go to the bathroom, the student raises the appropriate flag and an adult will respond.

Michael Pennington, who goes by the title of supervisor, is the only paid employee in this thirty-nine student school in Idabel, Oklahoma. He is assisted by a volunteer mother, who is called a monitor. They are in demand this particular afternoon. Several flags have gone up at once. The mother heads for a student who has a question about an upcoming field trip. Pennington goes to help a fourth-grade girl stymied by how to divide a number that will not divide evenly, such as five divided by two. Pennington pulls out some scratch paper and works several problems of division with remainders, then watches as the girl works a few in her A.C.E. workbook.

Satisfied that she understands the concept, he quickly walks to the other side of the room, where a junior high girl has raised a flag. The girl is ready to take a vocabulary test in her science workbook. Pennington reads definitions of eighteen words, one by one, and the girl correctly gives answers such as "anthracite" and "solstice." But she misses six of the eighteen, and Pennington tells her to keep studying. She can't proceed to the next page in the science workbook until she masters the vocabulary list.

The A.C.E. program is credited with much of the boom in fundamentalist Christian schooling. Dr. Donald R. Howard of Lewisville, Texas, thirty miles north of Dallas, started A.C.E. in 1970 to provide parents like himself an inexpensive alternative to public education. Howard is a former Baptist preacher who earned a doctorate in Christian education at Bob Jones University. Howard's wife, Esther, supervises layout and evaluates content in the A.C.E. curriculum. They became interested in alternative schools when their son failed first grade in the public schools.[1] They were soon joined in the endeavor by Dr. Ronald E. Johnson, who had been a public school principal and a member of the Arizona Governor's Commission on Textbooks. As the company's partners, Howard and Johnson own all of

---

[1]Nancy Daly, "The Genesis of a Program Built on Creation," *New York Times,* 26 April 1981, sec. 12, 18-19.

the stock and direct about 200 employees. The school-in-a-kit company has grown to a fifteen-million-dollars-a-year operation with outlets in fifty countries.[2]

A.C.E. offers one-step shopping for the church wanting to start a school. For just a few thousand dollars, A.C.E. can transform any pastor into the principal of his own Christian school in a matter of weeks. A.C.E. supplies the workbooks and tests and, for additional costs, even red-white-and-blue uniforms and pencil sharpeners so that no church has to deal with any secular educational firm.

The central tenet of Howard's system is the radical belief that teaching is not important in the learning process. Howard contends that children learn more effectively by working out of a book at their own speed than by listening to a teacher who, by necessity, must keep the class at a common plateau.

"It's a false premise that, because a body with a degree stands in front of a room and speaks words, learning is taking place," Johnson, A.C.E.'s Vice President for Development, told me during a visit to company headquarters. "It's a false assumption to believe that every child in that room is at the same level of understanding. There is no classroom of twenty-five children in which they are all at the same academic or maturity level. Chronological age does not determine academic level or maturity. Grading by age is simply an administrative convenience."

For years, schools have placed students in grades according to age. Of course, many schools also have ability groupings within classes. Johnson says this helps, but it still doesn't compare to A.C.E.'s individualized approach. Critics of that approach point out, however, that A.C.E.'s one-on-one is not between a student and a teacher a la Socrates, but between a student and a series of consumable workbooks. "A.C.E. reminds me of spending twelve years on a Timex assembly line. How dull," one teacher at a conventional Christian school said.

But A.C.E. isn't necessarily as bleak as it sounds. Pupils have a one-to-one relationship with the supervisor and the monitor on a regular basis. In fact, Johnson contends that A.C.E. has more individualized instruction than many conventional classrooms where a child may sit for weeks and never raise his hand or be called on by the teacher. In the A.C.E. program, the supervisor must continually check the progress of students for them to advance in their workbooks. Supervisors are prohibited from grading tests

---

[2]"Where God Is the Teacher," *Newsweek* (28 February 1983): 72.

or even from sitting at their desks during school hours. To encourage them to keep circulating in the classroom, the supervisor's desk has no chair.

The workbooks carry colorful cartoons featuring clean-cut, happy children with such names as Ace Virtueson and Christi Lovejoy. Unlike newspaper cartoons where characters stay the same age for years, Ace and Christi and the rest of the gang mature into responsible, soul-winning teenagers in the advanced workbooks. The supervisor in A.C.E.'s fictional "workbook school" is Mr. Friendson, the monitor is Miss Content, and the church leader is Pastor Alltruth. Even in the selection of character names, A.C.E. doesn't let pass an opportunity to moralize.

Let's now enact a typical day in these atypical schools with the help of Ace, Christi, and friends. The dramatization that follows is fictional, of course, but it adheres faithfully to the procedures used in A.C.E. schools nationwide. Whether the school is in Savannah or Seattle, these procedures are implemented with precision. The following, then, is a portrayal using the actual names of A.C.E.'s cast of characters and the actual guidelines contained in A.C.E.'s manual of procedures.

8:30 a.m.—Opening exercise.

Pastor Alltruth begins the school day with a song, a prayer and pledges to the American and Christian flags. Today, Reginald Upright and Sandy McMercy receive "congratulation slips" for their successful completion of a workbook the previous day.

The pastor tells the pupils their weekly field trip on Friday will be to the county courtroom. As his A.C.E. manual recommended, he already has checked to make sure the court session that day will not expose students to vice or pornography.[3] He provides motivation by reminding students that only those who complete their workbook goals will get to go on the field trip.

Pastor Alltruth keeps the opening exercise to fifteen minutes and makes it inspirational, not a time for preaching or for chewing out students such as Racer Loyalton, who showed up two minutes late and received a demerit as a result.

8:45 a.m.—Work time.

Ace, Christi, Reginald, Sandy, Racer, and the others promptly sit at their "offices"—individual study carrels that line the walls of a large room. It's like the fabled one-room schoolhouse of old, with children from ages

---

[3]*A.C.E. Procedures Manual*, rev. November 1982 (Lewisville TX: Accelerated Christian Education, Inc.) 116.

six to eighteen in the same room. To reduce distractions, no child is look-ing at another. All face a wall, with the teacher's desk and reference tables in the middle of the room. Students devote the first five minutes to silently reading Psalm 1, which is their Bible memorization passage for the month. By quoting the entire chapter, they can receive valuable free-time privi-leges.

Students then open their self-instructional workbooks as the supervi-sor, Mr. Friendson, gives tests, listens to oral reports, and explains to a group of children how to use a dictionary. The adult monitor, Miss Con-tent, goes from desk to desk checking whether each student met the pre-vious day's goals and has set new ones for today.

9:50 a.m.—Break.

After a solid hour in the workbooks, students take a five-minute break. Pudge Meekway looks at the clock and sighs. He wishes he had been more diligent last week. Students can earn longer breaks by meeting workbook goals. Miriam Peace, for example, gets a fifteen-minute morning break because she memorized the previous month's Bible selection, completed at least one and one-half workbooks per week, and maintained a good be-havior record. J. Michael Kindhart has an even better deal. He gets a twenty-five minute morning break and the privilege to be out of his seat without permission because he completed two workbooks per week and also presented a special oral report.

9:55 a.m.—Work time.

It's back to the workbooks, called PACEs for Packet of Accelerated Christian Education. Material for grades one through twelve is organized into 144 workbooks in each of five subjects: English, math, social studies, word building, and science. To advance at the normal rate, a student must complete an average of twelve workbooks a year in each subject for twelve years. That's sixty workbooks a year, or about one and one-half a week. If Pudge goes slower than that, he won't graduate by the age of eighteen. At the rate Reginald Upright is going, he could graduate at age sixteen and start college if he passes the entrance exams. Graduation from A.C.E. schools is based strictly on the amount of learning, not on age.

Each week, students map their own strategy for the PACE work. Pudge, for instance, committed himself to doing six pages a day in social studies, five a day in English, eight a day in science, and so on. He's working on one PACE in each subject, but the PACEs are on varying levels. He's at fourth-grade level in his favorite subject of math, but at a second-grade level in most of the other subjects. He particularly dislikes English, but Mr.

Friendson keeps after Pudge to meet his five-pages-a-day goal in the English PACE. Pupils are trained to see the attainment of daily goals as steps necessary to maintain continuous progress.

10:55 a.m.—Break.

Mr. Friendson and Miss Content encourage the children to go outside, weather permitting, at each break. Since the curriculum requires so much reading, the staff seeks to prevent vision problems. The A.C.E. manual says being outdoors relaxes the eyes by allowing a child to focus on distant objects. In addition, the manual recommends that students never be asked to read in front of a group because that might create muscle tension in the eyes. Also, Mr. Friendson conducts a one-minute eye exercise at the end of break time. Pupils hold their fists about twelve inches away and focus on their thumbs. Then they focus on an object on the far side of the room. Students quickly focus back and forth between the two points six times while the supervisor counts.

11 a.m.—Work time.

Ace, Christi, and their schoolmates return to their PACE work. Hapford Humblen, having already met his daily goals in English and math, is plugging away in his science workbook that teaches about quartz and other minerals. He reads the text, then answers questions about the text by filling in the blanks. He raises his flag to gain permission to go to the scorer's table, where he compares his answers with the scoring book. He returns to his "office," corrects his mistakes, raises his flag again, and rescores. The process continues until Hapford has all answers correct. He now can proceed to the next section in the workbook.

Meanwhile, Racer Loyalton is having a bad day. Miss Content caught him turning around in his chair and whispering to Christi. He gets a second demerit.

Noon—Lunch.

Students at most A.C.E. schools bring their own sack lunches, although a few schools offer lunches for modest prices. Diet is looked on as an important factor in learning. Racer, for instance, tends to be inattentive and hyperactive. Based on the A.C.E. manual, Pastor Alltruth has recommended to Mr. and Mrs. Loyalton that they restrict Racer from white sugar and flour, food coloring, canned goods, preservatives, candy, and soft drinks.

12:30 p.m.—Work time.

Booker Thriftway is nearing the end of his word-building PACE started three weeks earlier. He's read the text thoroughly, completed all checkups, and is ready to take the Self Test. The flag goes up, and Mr. Friendson gives Booker permission to take the Self Test. Booker grades his own test and makes a ninety-two—good enough to take the PACE Test that goes in Mr. Friendson's record book. The PACE Test is taken the morning after a pupil passes the Self Test, and Mr. Friendson grades it. Each PACE Test begins with the direction, "Ask Jesus to help you." Undoubtedly, this is a wise policy since Booker must make a ninety or better to advance to the next workbook in the series. If he makes an eighty-nine or below, he must start over in the same workbook, delaying his progress by a week or more.[4]

In each PACE, students have checkups along the way to measure their retention in small segments. The Self Test at the end of the workbook permits students to evaluate their total understanding. The PACE Test that follows is the supervisor's measurement of what the students have learned.

1:30 p.m.—Break.

This is a standard ten-minute break for everyone. The morning and early afternoon are devoted to working the PACEs. From here on, the day takes on a new character.

1:40 p.m.—Devotionals, P.E., and activities.

Pastor Alltruth leads devotions for teenagers while the children go outside to play. Later, the pastor conducts devotions for the children while the teenagers exercise outdoors.

A.C.E. recommends that a different character trait be presented each week in the devotionals. For example, Pastor Alltruth on Monday defines the character trait of "appreciation" and uses it in a biblical illustration. On Tuesday, he gives it a historical illustration, and on Thursday he applies it to practical living. Ace, Christi, and the others are required to keep a notebook of insights gained from the sessions.

Physical education activities include basketball, ping pong, and volleyball. Other activities may include music, arts and crafts, sewing, and auto mechanics. Unfortunately for Racer Loyalton, he was caught talking without permission during the devotional. A third demerit in the same day automatically means a twenty-minute detention.

2:50 p.m.—Cleanup.

Reginald Upright again breezed through his assigned number of pages today, but Pudge Meekway didn't fare so well. Pudge didn't meet his so-

---

[4]The minimum passing grade used to be 80, but the standard was raised for 3rd ed. PACEs. In A.C.E.'s monthly publication, *The Accelerator* (April 1983): 6, officials say the new passing grade of 90 is "not an indication that Third Edition is too easy." Instead, A.C.E. says it verifies that the self-directed system of learning is effective.

cial studies goal, and that means homework. Pudge requests a homework slip from Miss Content. The monitor marks the social studies pages that Pudge needs to complete that night to meet his daily goal, and Pudge's mother must sign the homework slip. Her signature does not verify the accuracy of Pudge's work or even that he will complete it. That is Pudge's responsibility. He knows if he doesn't do the work that night, he starts the next day in trouble.

Mr. Friendson fills out a detention slip for Racer, who will serve his time tomorrow after school. The detention slip he carries home today lets his parents know he will be staying twenty minutes late the next day as punishment.

Ace, Christi, and the others clean their desks during this time. PACEs are neatly stacked on the left side of the desk and pencils are placed in a container.

3:00 p.m.—End of school.

Mr. Friendson follows the suggestion of the training manual and sends the students home with a word of encouragement.

That's a typical day for Ace Virtueson, Christi Lovejoy, and friends. Although the time frames may differ somewhat, A.C.E. encourages conformity to this general structure on Mondays, Tuesdays, and Thursdays. Wednesdays are special chapel days that feature an hour-long religious service with a guest speaker, no PACE work, and an early dismissal. The A.C.E. manual says chapel speakers invited to the school should "avoid making favorable comments on or endorsements of television, secular movies, mixed swimming, teen dating, social drinking, Halloween, Santa Claus, or the Easter bunny."[5] Fridays consist of PACE work and a field trip for those who earned it. The A.C.E. manual gives guidelines on carefully screening field trip locales in advance to prevent exposing students to vulgarity or inappropriate behavior.

In its formative years, A.C.E. withstood a barrage of criticism that it represented educational humanism at its worst, since it placed the child at the center of his own learning environment. A.C.E. lived through that flurry of criticism with a defense that, actually, God is the teacher and the workbooks are mere instruments of learning.

The A.C.E. program still has its critics. One Christian textbook competitor groused: "Can you imagine sitting at a booth for twelve years and

---

[5]*A.C.E. Procedures Manual*, 99.

going to college that first day and the teacher starts rattling off? They won't be able to handle it.'' A.C.E. counters that its graduates going to college and confronting the lecture method are bored stiff. ''Kids are used to assuming their own pace, taking the responsibility,'' Johnson says. ''To have to sit through lectures, they're very, very bored.''

An Alabama educator on the A.C.E. system says the concept is great for self-motivated students, but he struggles constantly to prod the others into meeting their workbook goals. He has one sixteen-year-old doing fifth-grade work. ''Other students may feel they can slide down to that level,'' said David Pope, principal of Landmark Christian School in Montgomery. He also fears that the A.C.E. approach makes it easier to cheat. ''It's easy to look at the answer book and memorize the answers. The goal then becomes passing the test, and not learning.''

A.C.E. is aware of that possibility. In its procedures manual for supervisors, the company warns that students have been known to carry a pencil to the scoring table to copy from the answer book. A.C.E. has developed an elaborate system of pen-and-pencil precautions to prevent cheating. Students mark their goals chart in blue ink to prevent them from changing their daily goals once set. They work in their PACE workbooks in pencil since wrong answers are to be erased and corrected. At the stand-up scoring table, there is only a red pen. Students are told to take no writing utensils to the table since all answers are to be checked only in red ink. Finally, the supervisor uses a green ink pen to approve students' work. It is, presumably, the only green ink pen on the premises.

Shortcomings of the teacherless system to education can become particularly evident on the secondary level, where the subject matter gets more complex and perhaps over the head of the nonspecialist, all-purpose supervisor. When Robert Kenley became principal of the Glad Tidings Institute in Sherman, Texas, he found that about twenty high school students in the former A.C.E. school required remedial work. ''The students would ask the teachers questions about math,'' Kenley said, ''and the teachers didn't know what they were talking about because the questions were not answered in the packets.''[6] Many schools also supplement A.C.E. with writing assignments since the canned curriculum concentrates on regurgitation of information rather than on creative thinking.

Yet many fundamentalist pastors consider A.C.E. the greatest thing since, well, the McGuffey Readers. They are certainly on target with one

---

[6]''Where God Is the Teacher,'' *Newsweek* (28 February 1983): 72.

observation. Students cannot go through twelve years of the A.C.E. program and not be able to read. Since A.C.E. is book-oriented, children spend most of each day with their noses in the print.

"This is the traditional approach to education in America," says the Rev. Ron Caskey, founder of the Cherry Creek Baptist School in suburban Denver, one of eighty A.C.E. schools in Colorado. "Originally, education started with the preacher as teacher and the Bible as textbook." Adds Fred Corrie, principal of the Irvington Christian Academy in Houston: "The A.C.E. program opened the door. Every church can now afford to open a religiously oriented school in its own facilities."[7]

In Anchorage, Alaska, pastor Jerry Prevo bought the A.C.E. program and established a church school for sixty-five students in 1970. In less than a decade, it grew to 700 students and eighty staff members. Many A.C.E. schools are meager church-basement operations with a dozen or so pupils. Others operate out of homes, with mothers in charge. Then there are schools such as the one in Anchorage that have grown into thriving centers with hundreds of students. The average A.C.E. school starts with twenty-four pupils and has seventy-five students by the third year.

A.C.E. schools do not have entrance exams. No matter what the child's IQ, a pupil is welcome if his attitude is right. Pastors are repeatedly cautioned against accepting children with bad attitudes or teenagers with a history of drug or alcohol abuse. The key is whether there is a desire to change. Normally, an A.C.E. school will not accept a problem child who doesn't want to change.

Before a young child starts in the PACEs, he first goes through a learn-to-read program that takes nine weeks or longer. After that, the child takes a phonics test and, upon passing, advances to the first of more than 700 PACEs he must complete during the next twelve years. A pupil transferring from a public school is given a battery of diagnostic tests, not automatically placed on the PACE level corresponding to his grade level and age. A.C.E. contends that public school transfers frequently are one to two grade levels below the A.C.E. curriculum.

For every fifty students, a school is supposed to have one supervisor and two monitors. The supervisor doesn't necessarily have to have any educational experience. The monitors often are mothers who work for free in exchange for reduced tuition costs for their school-age children. The job

---

[7]Ibid.

description of supervisors and monitors is more than just keeping a lookout for raised flags. They are motivators as well.

"We believe in the therapy of touch," Johnson said. "We train the men supervisors to go by each boy's office and pat him on the shoulder, squeeze his shoulder a little bit, and say things like 'Son, I'm so glad to have you in the school. I appreciate you. I'm praying for you. I hope you're praying for me. How are you doing in your goals this week?' The women are taught to touch the girls in the same manner.

"The child's dependence on the adult person in the room is minimal, but the child's accountability is very high. The supervisor's responsibility is not to give the child information or answers or to lecture to him, but to control his environment and to motivate him so the child can let the material teach him."

A.C.E. schools emphasize the eyes as the source of learning, rather than the ears or the hands. "We are a paper society. We are not an oral transmission society," Johnson says. "The world is held together by typewriters, or I guess word processors now." Hence, the emphasis in these teacherless schools is on *reading* workbooks, not *hearing* a teacher or *doing* experiments.

Students in these teacherless schools are free to choose between the college-prep or the vocational diploma routes, and many of them choose the easier vocational route. A.C.E. headquarters encourages member schools to push the college-prep curriculum that emphasizes algebra, geometry, literature, and the sciences. Johnson says sixty percent of A.C.E. graduates go on to college—mostly to Bible colleges—or other special training.

Pastors on their way to becoming A.C.E. school principals are required to come to Lewisville, Texas, for a week of intensive training. No Lewisville training, no school. The pastors, their wives, and the supervisors-to-be are treated during the week just like students. Each is given an "office" in the training room. The adults receive demerits if they fail to push their chairs in properly after getting up. They spend hours working in Training PACEs, learning how the teacherless system operates.

"The difference between a good school and a bad one is the man at the helm," Johnson says. "Bad schools are usually run by men without A.C.E. training or who lack a commitment to A.C.E.'s ways of instruction." It seldom happens, but a church school that violates A.C.E.'s strict procedures can be stripped of permission to use company materials.

Trainees are given a tour of the A.C.E. headquarters, located on 129 acres that once was a doctor's farm in the middle of rolling Texas prairie.

Like any big business, there are rooms full of computers and video display terminals that keep track of school orders. This is a substantial business enterprise.

In the distribution area, boxes roll down an assembly line on their way to schools from coast to coast. At the time I visited, seven boxes containing 1,242 PACES were being prepared for delivery to Groton Christian Academy in Groton, Massachusetts. A.C.E. tries to keep a backlog of some sixteen million PACEs in storage.

Another room contains uniforms and supplies, ranging from staplers to softballs to the six-inch Christian-and-American flag sets selling for $1.30. One long shelf is crammed with ties of all shapes and sizes. There are big ones for adults and little ones for children. There are straight ties and bow ties. There are kerchiefs for women and girls. They all have one common characteristic: they are red, white, and blue with tiny American flags on them. Want to keep abreast of the latest fundamentalist fashion? An A.C.E. shipping clerk confided: ''The big bow ties are out of style and aren't being made anymore. The little bow ties for boys, though, are growing in popularity. Bow ties are coming back.''

Everyone, literally everyone, inside A.C.E. headquarters wears the patriotic uniforms, from the shipping clerks to the secretaries to the company president. The entire complex is splashed in patriotic colors.

Lewisville Christian Academy is housed in a nearby domed structure. Many of the students are the offspring of A.C.E. employees. Like their parents, each day they wear the standard God-and-country uniforms. Their tiny ''offices'' are neat. A Bible rests on each desk, and Ronald Reagan buttons adorn several bulletin boards. The supervisor's desk, looking straight out of a spaceship movie, is a round ''command center'' in the middle of the round room. The darkened domed ceiling features Christmas tree lights that depict the Texas sky on a clear night in March.

After touring the headquarters and observing the model school in action, pastors and supervisors return again to their PACE work. The week of training is strictly regimented. Finally, they get to pepper A.C.E. Vice President Lewis Bridges with questions they've been wanting to ask all week. I unobtrusively attended one of the Q&A sessions for pastors and supervisors representing sixty churches in the United States and Canada. Here's how it went:

Q: Does a church need to get a zoning change to start a school?
A: My advice is to not let local officials zone you for a school, but stay zoned as a church. You're not starting a school. You're extending the educational ministry of your church to weekdays.

Q: Should you take in children to your school who aren't saved?

A: Be very careful about taking an unsaved teen into your school. He can be a corrupting influence on the others.

Q: If Jesus taught by the lecture method, why not use it in schools?

A: Christ taught principles, not academics. There's some merit in conventional teaching, if students with the same mentality are having the same problems at the same time. Chances are, though, this won't be the case. The conventional class teaches only to the average student.

Q: Is it possible not to charge tuition but to build in extra contributions to the church?

A: That would depend on which IRS bureaucrat you talked to.

Q: How do you decide what hours to hold school?

A: You as the pastor or principal set the hours. I believe in having school as much as possible. I don't like the four-day week. At Lewisville Christian Academy, kids go to school from 8 a.m. to 4:30 p.m. I'd have them go on Saturdays, too, if it was possible. They also go year-round. School used to end in summer so kids could work in the fields when we were an agricultural society. Now, summer is just for kids getting into trouble.

Q: I've heard A.C.E. hits the doctrine of eternal security pretty hard in its curriculum. Is that true?

A: No. This doctrine is a point where good men differ, so we don't deal with that.

Q: What do you think of home schools?

A: A lot of prominent Christian leaders are pushing home schools. We don't. Most parents do not have the commitment or the character to do this. God has provided a place to send the child—a place to delegate that responsibility.

Q: What do you do with a six- or seven-year-old who does not want to read?

A: Don't make him read. Wait for him to grow up more.

Q: What are the qualifications for your curriculum writers?

A: We're interested in Bible college graduates, not from secular schools.

Q: Does A.C.E. have dress slacks for girls?

A: No. Have you ever seen a lady in a pair of slacks? The answer is no. When a woman gets in a pair of slacks, she ceases to be a lady. Ladies, if you want to show your form to the wicked, lustful eyes of the wicked world, you're not ladylike.

The room was filled with "amens" on that point, and so ended the uninhibited question-and-answer session at A.C.E. headquarters—the birthplace of some 5,000 schools responsible for educating half a million children in America today.

THE DISTINCTIVES: BACK TO THE OLD WAYS

Girls who perform as athletes or cheerleaders in the presence of males soon lose their inhibitions. They become calloused about immodesty. Their sense of purity is weakened. Boys who watch females during aggressive athletic or cheering activity find their thoughts drifting from interest in the game to interest in the girls. Even the purest boy cannot for long cast his eyes upon physically active girls without experiencing fleeting or lingering thoughts not directly related to the sport taking place.

Dr. Ronald E. Johnson
Accelerated Christian Education
Lewisville, Texas

7

ADAM AND EVE VERSUS CHARLES DARWIN

The Bible opens with these simple words: "In the beginning God created the heaven and the earth."

Genesis tells of a creation that took six days, culminating in the formation of man from the dust of the earth and the formation of woman from a rib of the man. We have our first parents, Adam and Eve, in the splendor of the garden of Eden.

History? Science? Folklore?

A Gallup Poll asked Americans their views on the origin of life. The results revealed the deeply religious nature of the American people. Gallup found that forty-four percent of those polled accept the Genesis account of creation as having occurred within the past 10,000 years. Another thirty-eight percent believe that although man evolved from lower life forms across millions of years, God directed the process. Another nine percent believe in an evolution in which God had no part, and the remaining nine percent said they did not have a belief.[1]

If eighty-two percent of Americans believe that God guided the creation of mankind, and if more than half of that eighty-two percent reject any kind of evolutionary process, it is small wonder that the century-old dispute over evolution remains alive.

In fundamentalist schools, creation is taught as the truth and evolution is taught as fiction. These schools emphasize to students that scientists weren't around at the beginning of time, so no one could possibly know how the earth began or how mankind began. The creation, after all, was a one-time event. It can't be tested in a laboratory.

"The Bible is without doubt scientifically accurate," states a Christian school science textbook. "Because God is its author, we can depend upon it to be true, accurate, and unchanging. It sometimes takes science many years to catch up with the Bible, but true science and the Bible are always in perfect agreement."[2]

Few issues in our time so clearly delineate the basic difference in belief systems between fundamentalist Christians and others. Many Americans wonder why attacking the theory of evolution is so important to fundamentalists. It's important because they view the evolutionist concept as striking at the very heart of their faith. As a Christian school textbook states:

> If man is nothing more than a highly evolved animal, then he is to be congratulated for his struggle upward and is to be excused when he acts like an animal; but if man is the divinely created being the Bible tells us he is, then man is a creature made in the image of God and a sinner in need of divine grace.[3]

---

[1]Richard Severo, "Poll Finds Americans Split on Creation Idea," *New York Times,* 29 August 1982, 22. The statement accepted by 44% of the 1,518 randomly selected respondents said: "God created man pretty much in his present form at one time within the last 10,000 years." The statement accepted by 38% of the respondents said: "Man has developed over millions of years from less advanced forms of life, but God guided this process, including man's creation." Nine percent agreed with the statement: "Man has developed over millions of years from less advanced forms of life. God had no part in this process." The remaining 9% had no opinion. The Gallup organization said the margin of error was 3%.

[2]*Science: Matter & Motion* (Pensacola FL: A Beka Book Publications, 1981) 76.

[3]Ibid., 493.

The origin of humankind, then, is considered crucial because it is here that the latest reaches of science touch a most ancient source of faith. The origin of human life often is viewed as having only two sides—creation versus evolution. Actually, there are many mediating positions on evolution, the relation between evolution and theism, and even the nature of theism itself. Yet in order to set the stage for the fundamentalist and non-fundamentalist Christian perspectives to follow, let's consider a reductionist model of naturalism versus theism. Naturalism discounts the supernatural and believes that scientific laws can account for all phenomena. Theism accepts the supernatural and believes in the existence of one God who, as creator of all, transcends yet is immanent in the world. This is one way of looking at it:

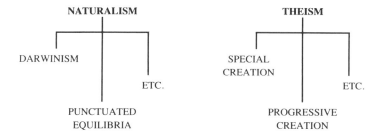

As one form of naturalism, there is Darwinism with its slow, step-by-step evolutionary process. Another form is the punctuated equilibria theory, which holds that periodic environmental upheaval hastens the creation of species. The "Etc." recognizes the many other theories that seek to explain "missing links" in the process, but always within a context that dismisses a supernatural presence.

On the other side are those who believe in a creator. One form of theism is the fundamentalist view of a special creation some 6,000 years ago. Another form is the belief in a progressive creation, which accepts evolution as the method God chose to do his creating. There are alternate views as well, but all theistic models share the common belief in a creator.

Advocates of evolution, then, are on both sides. In this reductionist model, naturalists accept evolution without God; theists accept evolution as from God.

The vast majority of Christian schools teach the special-creation concept. They object to the portrayal of man as merely something that evolved by accident from amino acids and a series of mutations. They object to the idea that our ancestors crawled out of the ocean and evolved into a two-legged creature over eons of time. Some fundamentalists go so far as to estimate, based on family lines listed in the Bible, that human life is only 6,000 years old. They believe in a literal Adam and Eve.

"We live in an evolution-crazed world," states a reference guide for science teachers in Christian schools. "We are told that everything we see—stars, galaxies, planets, and living organisms, including man himself—has evolved spontaneously out of primordial self-existent matter, is still evolving, and will continue to evolve in the future. . . . Such fanciful theorizing is both unscriptural and unscientific."[4]

The American Association of Christian Schools places the issue in an even broader context. In a brochure, AACS President A. C. Janney warns parents of the consequences of placing their children in the public schools where evolution is taught:

> Evolution is more than just a matter of where we came from; it's a whole attitude toward truth. Evolution says that we have simply evolved to a higher species of life from a lower, that evolution has a migration of truth, that is to say, that truth means one thing one day and something else the next. It is very important that we take a good look at this particular point. The Bible says, "Jesus Christ is the same yesterday, and today, and for ever." Anybody who teaches anything less than that is teaching wrong, but your children, for the most part, are taught that there are no absolute truths.[5]

The nonfundamentalist Christian schools scoff at placing the theory of evolution in such a broad context. To them, the theistic view of a progressive creation is a viable theory. They say God could have used evolution as his way of creating life. Needless to say, special creationists have little regard for the views of the progressive creationists, and vice versa.

Dr. Frank H. Roberts teaches science at Delaware County Christian School in Pennsylvania. While his ninth-graders busily melted galena at their lab stations, Roberts took a moment to discuss how he handles the sensitive subject of origins. "Among Christians," Roberts said, "there's a wide range of opinion from the assumption that anything that takes evolution into account is totally false all the way to the other extreme that evolution is the way God created the world. My approach as teacher is to show this wide spectrum. Evolution has been a healthy theory for one hundred years. I do not think anyone with his head screwed on can reach the con-

---

[4]"The Christian Teaching of Science" (pamphlet by BJU Press, 1981) 14.

[5]A. C. Janney, "Who Me?" (an undated brochure published by the American Association of Christian Schools) 2.

clusion that the world was created in 6,000 years. But the real issue is whether there's a God or not. The world is hungry, pollution is overtaking us, people are dying without salvation. That's far more important than whether the world is 6,000 years old. My relationship with God isn't dependent on how old I think the world is.''

Following the Bible's opening statement of God's creation of the heavens and earth, Genesis 1:2 states, ''And the earth was without form, and void.''

Dr. Philip Elve, now retired from the nonfundamentalist Christian Schools International in Grand Rapids, Michigan, points out that the earth existed for an undetermined time before God formed man and woman. ''We strictly believe in creation. But Genesis 1 is not a textbook,'' Elve said. ''It doesn't have all the details. There's a lot we can only speculate about. And to say 'Now you've got to believe in 6,000 years' when the Bible doesn't say that, well, you can believe in that if you want to. Another may believe that when the earth was void, there was a long, long millions and even billions of years at that point.''

Genesis 1:3 says: ''And God said, Let there be light; and there was light.''

Harvard astrophysicist Owen Gingerich is a Christian who believes in evolution. He places the age of the earth at ten to twenty billion years, and he is a proponent of the ''Big Bang'' theory of earth's creation. He says the Big Bang theory squares perfectly with God's words of ''Let there be light.'' In a guest lecture on ''Modern Cosmogony and Biblical Creation'' at the University of North Carolina, Gingerich soared into the far reaches of astrophysics and then talked about how his life's work and his faith have meshed. ''The universe is like a tapestry,'' Gingerich told the several hundred people present. ''You cannot undo one thread without upsetting the design. Can we not see the creator's hand at work?'' The astrophysicist said his ''leap of faith'' to Jesus Christ has placed science in a wholly new perspective for him. ''Science is, by its very nature, godless,'' he said. ''Genesis studies 'who' while science studies 'how.' I don't necessarily see a conflict between the two.''

But many people do. The conflict between Genesis and science emerged from the publication of Charles Darwin's book, *Origin of Species,* in 1859. Darwin theorized that higher forms of life evolved from lower forms through a process of mutation and natural selection. A mutant fish, for example, might form legs, which would give it an advantage since it then could survive in environments that might not support normal fish. Darwin believed in the ''survival of the fittest.'' In 1871, in *The Descent of Man,*

Darwin revealed his theory concerning the origin of man: "The Simiadae then branched off into two great stems, the New World and the Old World Monkeys; and from the latter, at a remote period, Man, the wonder and glory of the Universe, proceeded."[6]

The eventual showdown between Genesis and science came in 1925 in the small town of Dayton, Tennessee. A high school biology teacher named John T. Scopes had been arrested for teaching evolution. This violated a state law prohibiting the teaching of "any theory that denies the story of the divine creation of man as taught in the Bible and to teach instead that man had descended from a lower order of animals."[7]

The Scopes trial brought evolution to the national forefront. It was a battle of the old versus the new, the Genesis account versus modern science, the nineteenth century versus the twentieth. A Chicago trial lawyer named Clarence Darrow led Scopes's defense. The chief prosecutor was populist William Jennings Bryan, a superb orator and three-time candidate for president. Bryan's lack of knowledge about biology and sometimes even about the Bible made him a target for Darrow's ridicule. Although Scopes was found guilty and fined one hundred dollars, Darrow's defense of Darwin's theory was the victor in the public eye. Weary and discouraged, Bryan died five days after the trial ended.

The public had passed judgment, and science had won. Evolution became accepted doctrine. Textbooks were revised to reflect Darwin's theory as fact. And so it has stayed until only recently, when fundamentalists became activists in textbook adoption proceedings, in legislative halls and in courtrooms.

The most prominent creationism trial since Scopes took place in Arkansas in 1981.[8] The state legislature that year had passed a creation-science bill that required "balanced treatment" of the creation and evolution theories in public schools. The law did not require the teaching of crea-

---

[6]Charles Darwin, *The Descent of Man* (New York: The Modern Library, 1936) 528.

[7]The Tennessee law had been adopted in 1920 because the teaching of evolution was gaining acceptance in classrooms in other states. The last state law prohibiting the teaching of evolution in public schools was ruled unconstitutional by the Mississippi Supreme Court in 1970.

[8]I was state broadcast editor of the Associated Press in Arkansas during the creationism trial. For this discussion, I have relied on my files from that period and on daily summaries from the *New York Times*. For an overview of the trial, see *Creationism, Science, and the Law: The Arkansas Case,* ed. Marcel C. LaFollette (Cambridge MA: The MIT Press, 1983).

tionism, but it did require anyone teaching the evolution theory to give equal time to the creation theory. The law defined the concepts in this manner:

Creation-science	Evolution-science
1. Sudden creation of the universe, energy, and life from nothing.	1. Emergence of universe from disordered matter and emergence of life from non-life.
2. Insufficiency of mutation and natural selection in bringing about development of all living kinds from a single organism.	2. Sufficiency of mutation and natural selection in bringing about development of present living kinds from simple earlier kinds.
3. Changes only within fixed limits of originally created kinds of plants and animals.	3. Emergence by mutation and natural selection of present living kinds from simple earlier kinds.
4. Separate ancestry for man and apes.	4. Emergence of man from a common ancestry with apes.
5. Explanation of earth's geology by catastrophism, including the occurrence of a worldwide flood.	5. Explanation of the earth's geology and the evolutionary sequences by uniformitarianism.
6. Relatively recent inception of the earth and living kinds.	6. Inception several billion years ago of the earth and somewhat later for life.

The American Civil Liberties Union contended that the creation-science theory was a smokescreen for teaching the Genesis account of creation. Arkansas Attorney General Steve Clark, not known as a conservative, found himself in the election-year position of having to defend the state law in federal court.

The fireworks began immediately. Evangelist Pat Robertson said on his "700 Club" telecast that Clark might be trying to lose the case. Robertson revealed that the state attorney general recently had contributed to a money-raising auction by the Arkansas chapter of the ACLU. Robertson likened Clark's activity to that of a boxer "taking a dive," adding, "It's like bribing a jury almost." Clark called the evangelist's accusations "absurd and asinine." Clark's donation to the ACLU auction was an offer to take the highest bidder to lunch. He said he had made similar contributions to a number of groups. Still, Clark found himself on the defensive in a case he really didn't want to defend.

Creationists sought to show that their "science" was as good as Darwin's. But the state's case started disastrously. The first witness, theology professor Norman Geisler of Dallas, asserted there was nothing necessarily religious about God. He said a discussion of God was religious only when accompanied by faith and could otherwise be dealt with as philosophy or history. Then, under cross-examination, Geisler acknowledged—amid courtroom laughter—that he believed in UFOs as "Satanic manifestations."

Next, a key witness for the state checked out of his hotel room overnight and left no word where he could be reached. The witness, Professor Dean Kenyon of San Francisco State University, had met with state attorneys the night before and was scheduled to testify the next day. Wendell Bird, general counsel for the fundamentalist Institute for Creation Research in San Diego, said he had advised Kenyon and ten other witnesses that the state was ill-prepared to defend the law. He said Kenyon left abruptly after sitting through a day's proceedings and being "absolutely horrified" at the state's defense actions. "I was not trying to sabotage the trial," Bird said. "The state was doing a totally inadequate job." Clark contended that Bird's actions undermined the state's effectiveness. "It not only means we were thrown to the wolves, but that the people who pretended to be interested in what we were doing really weren't," the attorney general said.

The state's best scientific witness was astronomer Chandra Wickramasinghe of Cardiff, Wales, who scoffed at the contention that natural selection could explain the appearance of the human race. He said the odds are infinitesimal that random shuffling of nucleic acid codes for each of the 2,000 genes controlling life processes would have produced human life. He likened it to the probability that "a tornado sweeping through a junkyard might assemble a Boeing 747."

U.S. District Judge William Overton continually pressed for scientific arguments in favor of teaching creation on an equal basis with evolution. He wanted pro-creation arguments, not anti-evolution arguments. Unsatisfied at the end, the judge declared the Arkansas law unconstitutional, calling it "simply and purely an effort to introduce the biblical version of creation into the public school curricula." The judge added: "The creationists do not take data, weigh it, and thereafter reach conclusions. Instead, they take the literal wording of Genesis and attempt to find scientific support for it."[9]

Since then, a creationist law enacted in Louisiana also has been declared unconstitutional, the governor of Arizona vetoed a bill that would

---

[9]McLean v. Arkansas, 529 F. Supp. 1255 (Eastern District, Arkansas, 1982). The state law itself was Act 590 of 1981.

have required the origin of life to be taught as "theory," and creationist bills failed to pass in the legislatures of Connecticut, Mississippi, and West Virginia.

While creationists have been losing the fight in legislative halls and in courts, they have been winning the fight in textbooks. It's not that creationist views are making it into public school textbooks. There is little evidence of that. But today's textbook publishers, to avoid a controversy that could doom sales, have been reducing or deleting references to evolution.

Texas is the bellwether state for creationists. In Texas, only five books in each subject are approved for adoption by the state. Because Texas is the world's biggest single buyer of textbooks, the State Board of Education's adoption requirements have great influence on what is made available to the rest of the country. To tap the state's sixty-four-million-dollar textbook bonanza, many publishers tailor their books for acceptance in Texas. As a result, textbooks in other states have the Texas brand on them.

For ten years, the Texas Board of Education required all biology textbooks used in the public schools to describe evolution as "only one of several explanations" of the origin of human beings. In 1984, the board reluctantly repealed the rule after the state attorney general questioned its constitutionality.[10] Still, the Texas rule has made an indelible print on biology textbooks across the nation.

Some publishers now put the chapter on Darwin in the back of the book so that teachers may ignore it or simply not get to it. A 1981 biology textbook, *Experiences in Biology,* by Laidlaw Brothers, omits the word "evolution" and makes no mention of Charles Darwin. The firm's director of publications, Eugene Frank, said, "We wanted teachers to be permitted to teach biology without being forced to face controversy from pressure groups." In 1982, the New York City public schools even rejected three textbooks from consideration, saying they gave inadequate treatment to the Darwin theory of evolution. The Laidlaw book was one of those rejected. Gerald Skoog of the Texas Tech College of Education has submitted standard textbooks to rigorous computer analysis. The results, he said, show a significant reduction in the amount of coverage given the evolutionary theory. In addition, scientific statements became less definite in later edi-

---

[10]"Anti-evolution Rules Are Unconstitutional," *Science* (30 March 1984): 1373; and "Texas Drops Requirement of Evolution as Theory," *Publishers Weekly* (27 April 1984): 19.

tions.[11] Even the definition of "science" was revised in one textbook from "total knowledge of facts and principles governing our lives, the world and everything in it" to "one way of discovering and interpreting" these facts and principles.[12]

The movement started in Texas has spread to other states. Here are public textbook revisions accepted by the California Board of Education in the 1970s to avoid evolutionary assumptions and to reduce scientific dogmatism:[13]

Original	Revised
Scientists believe life may have begun from amino acids or viruses, neither of which is usually considered living. Scientists believe life may have been transported from another planet.	Scientists do not know how life began on earth. Some suggest that life began from nonliving material. Others suggest that life may have been transported from another planet.
Plants took to the land and conquered it.	Plants appeared on the land.
Scientists can reconstruct the (prehistoric) animal. . . .	Scientists do their best to reconstruct the (prehistoric) animal. . . .
Slowly, over millions of years, the dinosaurs died out.	Slowly, the dinosaurs died out.
Paleontologists have been able to date the geological history of North America.	Paleontologists have assembled a tentative outline of the geological history of North America.

Some Christian schools still use secular textbooks. They like the rigorous academic content, although they may not like the tone or philosophy of the books. But not many go as far as the Memphis school that one year stamped "POISON" on each page of the evolution chapter in its secular biology text. The principal of the school said he liked the creationism emphasis in Christian textbooks, but "we couldn't find the 'science' we wanted, so we decided we could handle that one chapter on evolution."

Conversely, Christian school textbooks place all scientific discovery in a biblical context. As William S. Pinkston Jr. writes in BJU Press's *Bi-*

---

[11]"Texts for Today," *Scientific American* (March 1984): 64; and "Creationists Are Gaining Some Ground in the Textbook Battle," *Christianity Today* (22 October 1982): 70-71.

[12]"The Science Textbook Controversies," *Scientific American* (April 1976): 38.

[13]Ibid.

ology for Christian Schools: "The people who have prepared this book have tried consistently to put the word of God first and science second."

Beka, in particular, works hard to show a religious basis for scientific discovery. A Beka science textbook teaches that Galileo gained insight into the understanding of nature from the Bible. It teaches that Johann Kepler, a German Lutheran who devised the laws of planetary motion, was "inspired by his confidence in the God of the Bible." It teaches that Sir Isaac Newton "was a devout Christian who studied for the ministry but devoted his life to science because he believed that he could bring more glory to God in his generation if he could prove that the universe is operated by laws instituted by a rational, logical, benevolent Creator."[14]

This biblical foundation directs the scientific discovery all the way from the creation to the great flood. Let us look at how Beka textbooks handle these topics from a fundamentalist perspective.[15]

Creation of world:
From genealogies of the Old and New Testaments, we determine that the first humans spoken of in the Bible were created about 6,000 years ago. The whole sum of human history has transpired in this relatively short period of time. The earth and the universe may well be older than this, but no one knows for sure. Many people believe that God created the original matter and energy of the universe and then let it alone until He was ready to fashion the world as we know it today. This would perhaps explain the apparent great age we see here and there in the universe.

Creation of animals:
Some scientists say that the reptiles lived first and the mammals came later, but there is much evidence against this idea, which is based on the false teaching of evolution. From the Bible, we know that they were all created about 6,000 years ago.

Dinosaurs:
Some of the animals of North America that became extinct long ago were the dinosaurs—called dragons in Scripture. . . . We know that dinosaurs lived at the same time as man, because dinosaur tracks and human tracks

---

[14]*Science: Matter & Motion*: Galileo, 12-13; Kepler, 11; Newton, 23.

[15]"Creation of world" from *Science: Matter & Motion,* 33. The remainder of the topics from Beka's *New World History and Geography in Christian Perspective* (Pensacola FL: A Beka Book Publication, 1982): creation of animals, 63; dinosaurs, 63; great flood, 78-79; human migration, 3; continents, 5, new varieties, 78-79.

have been found together in the same rock layer.[16]

The Great Flood:
Someone has calculated that there are 114,637 different kinds of land animals in the world. How could all those animals fit into the Ark? The answer is easy when you consider that 100,000 of the kinds are insects! The remainder . . . could all fit easily into nests and stalls built on just one deck of the Ark. (The Ark was perhaps half the length of a modern ocean liner and much more roomy inside.) That would leave two decks free for storing food and supplies.

Human migration:
Over four thousand years ago, after the Great Flood of Noah's day, God caused the people of the world to speak many different languages and thus to spread out over all the earth.

Continents:
Many people believe . . . that South America and Africa were at one time a single landmass. If you check the world map, you can see how the two continents could fit together almost like pieces of a puzzle. The continents possibly could have been divided during the days of Noah's great-great-great-grandson Peleg, who was born 101 years after the Flood. Peleg's name means "divided," and the Bible says that "in his days the earth was divided" (Genesis 10:25).

New varieties:
God gave most kinds of animals an amazing ability to form new varieties. In the state of California alone, there are 33 different varieties of pocket gophers. They have all developed from just one pair of pocket gophers that left the Ark.

Christian school textbooks take continual swipes at Darwin. In discussing the Indians who live on the Tierra del Fuego islands off the southern tip of South America, Beka writes:

> They had a very simple and primitive way of life. Because of this, when the evolutionist Charles Darwin saw them during his voyage around South America, he mistakenly thought he had found a missing link between man and ape! He had actually found a group of people who had wandered so

---

[16]This is a reference to the Paluxy riverbed in Texas. At the time this Christian school textbook was written, creationists believed human footprints had been found among dinosaur prints in the Paluxy riverbed. Experts subsequently concluded that the "mantracks" apparently were made by a previously unknown kind of bipedal dinosaur that walked not on its toes, as other dinosaurs did, but on its heel and sole, thereby leaving faint toeprints. The Institute of Creation Research has withdrawn its book on the subject and has removed a display of the "mantracks" from its museum. See "The Case of the Mystery Footprints: A Clear Victory for Evolutionists," *Discover* (August 1986): 8, 10.

far away from God and other people that they had lost most of their culture and religious heritage.

After the world was made aware of Tierra del Fuego Indians, people became burdened to tell the Indians about Christ. . . . After many years of Christian witness, over 4,500 Indians (all but eight of them) became Christians. Their lives were so greatly changed that even Darwin admitted his mistake and gave money to the missionary work.

The Indians of Tierra del Fuego became very active for the Lord. They collected large amounts of money for other missionaries around the world, and they sent some of their own people as missionaries to other tribes. They were not half animals as Darwin had thought, but ordinary men who needed to hear the gospel.[17]

Christian school textbooks strive not to come across as antiscience. They portray science as vital to the understanding of God's world, but they attack the infallibility that scientific findings often are accorded. Still, as critics point out, Christian school textbooks devote far more space to attacks on evolution than to scientific evidence supporting creation.

The last chapter of one particular Beka science book is entitled "Science Versus Evolution." It devotes thirty-eight pages to a systematic attack of evolution, using as proof everything from the living cell to the second law of thermodynamics. The authors detail how "true science" refutes evolution from the standpoint of comparative anatomy, embryology, parasitology, taxonomy, paleontology, and genetics. The chapter concludes by saying: "We have seen that evolution is not really science. It may be classified as a religion or a philosophy, but it is not science. As a matter of fact, evolution is antiscience; it is a threat to modern science."[18]

There is an irony in Christian school textbooks purporting to be more scientifically true than secular school texts. The irony is that fundamentalists appear to have capitulated to the same agenda that the secularists have—namely, they both accept the concept of empirical science as an arbiter of truth. This emphasis on acquiring scientific support for creationism seems strangely out of place among a people who seek to live by faith based on absolute truths.

---

[17]*New World History and Geography in Christian Perspective,* 198.

[18]*Science: Matter & Motion,* 527. For a debate, see "The Genesis War," *Science Digest* (October 1981): 82-87. Duane Gish, director of the Institute for Creation Research, debates author/evolutionist Isaac Asimov.

8

SEX EDUCATION WITH MORALIZING

Sex education in Christian schools, if offered at all, comes packaged in strict absolutist language. Christian schools teach that the biblical thou-shalt-nots about premarital sex, adultery, divorce, and homosexuality still apply in twentieth century America. Students are not encouraged to develop their own moral code. Instead, a moral code based on the Bible is given them as Truth.

Some Christian schools refuse to have anything hinting of sex education in their curriculum. They consider it a topic strictly for the home. Other schools offer the basics of sex education, but without using that charged terminology. Sex education is incorporated into "health studies" on the elementary level and through "Bible" or "family life" classes on the secondary level.

"We feel it's important to teach sex education," says Stephen Dill of Delaware County Christian School in Newtown Square, Pennsylvania. "I teach a Bible class for eleventh graders. It's on marriage and family, on the responsibility of husbands and wives. We deal with dating, petting, physical involvement, sex, divorce, everything."

Dill said he allows students to lead round-robin discussions rather than listen to a lecture, but the discussions always must be within a moral framework. "I do steer the discussion," he said. "For instance, the scripture teaches that premarital intercourse is wrong, so there are conclusions I want them to reach."

Christian school leaders object to the teaching of sex education apart from God and his standard of morality as viewed through the Bible. They despair that moral relativism and situational ethics have supplanted God's standard of morality. "Teaching sex apart from God's view of sex can only lead to a perversion of sex and sink our youth into a morass of immorality," writes the Rev. Calvin Cummings, founder of Trinity Christian School in Pittsburgh.[1]

Christian school educators believe the public schools are wrong in teaching sex education outside a moral framework. They argue that the public schools don't teach right and wrong, but instead teach freedom of choice. This, they say, is moral relativism and situational ethics as opposed to absolute truths. They believe the emphasis in sex education classes at the public schools is more on contraception than on abstention.

"They're trying to make sexual animals of our children," declared an angry Tim LaHaye, who has written extensively on sexual topics from a fundamentalist perspective. "Mixed classes shouldn't be talking about intercourse, erections, and all that. Any teacher who would do such a thing has to be so bereft of moral standards that he'd have to be considered mentally sick."

The sex education message delivered in Christian schools is far different from the public schools' nonjudgmental approach. At the Southern Baptist Educational Complex in Memphis, I visited a sex education class that goes by the name of "Marriage and Family." The thirteen class members used a book on dating as a springboard to a class discussion on dating

---

[1]Calvin K. Cummings, "Parents," *The Purpose of a Christian School* (Phillipsburg NJ: Presbyterian and Reformed Publishing Co., 1979) 13.

practices. Mrs. Brown let the teenagers do the talking before she casually suggested praying with a date sometime. She laughed and added, "Now isn't that about the old-fogiest, old-fashionest idea you've ever heard?" She asked if any of them had ever done so. No one had, but some of the seventeen-year-old girls thought it was a good idea.

Mrs. Brown led the discussion in a relaxed manner, occasionally spouting traditional theories of sex and marriage without coming across as preachy or condescending. "The 'I do' in a marriage is for life. *For life,*" she said with emphasis the second time. "I've been married thirty-two years and love keeps growing. 'Being in love' is not love. It's a stage toward love. When the honeymoon ends—and I define that as when the couple has its first real fight—it's vital that a couple handle the disillusionment to follow." Mrs. Brown looked at some of the girls in a class. "Because you'll find yourself saying, 'You mean I'm going to have to spend the rest of my life with *him?*' "

Mrs. Brown said a couple must share a spiritual, mental, and emotional commitment before the wedding. If in doubt, call it off. She suggested a one-year engagement to allow both parties to be certain they have met their life's partner. She told the class the fourth area of commitment—physical—will be hard to avoid before marriage but that it is important to maintain sexual purity. "And forget the bachelor's party, guys. You don't need the lewd movies and stray girls," she said as the guys in the class grinned at her good-naturedly.

Four of the thirteen students in this class came from broken homes. One year, three-fourths of her class came from divorced families. "The divorce rate has become so astronomical that I decided to meet it head-on," Mrs. Brown said. She regularly talks in class about the dilemma of divorce. She tells the class that children of divorced parents tend to get divorced themselves because they lack a "trust pattern" from their parents. She wants those from broken homes to be aware of that dilemma so that, when they get married, they will strive to break that cycle.

In this 720-student school, two girls have become pregnant the past four years, both by boys outside the school. Both girls automatically were dismissed from school. Principal Paul Young said he had never been confronted with a situation where he knew a boy in his school had impregnated a girl, so he didn't know how he would handle that situation.

"But I'm afraid we'll see more and more of these problems," Young said. "I think we're going to see homosexuality in our schools. I really believe those of us in Christian education are going to be sorry one day that we said, 'Come here and be protected.' As the world becomes stronger, as it already is, it will creep more into our schools.''

To combat that possibility, the strictest fundamentalist schools simply prohibit physical contact between boys and girls. These schools have what is popularly called "the six-inch rule" that requires boys and girls to stay six inches apart. The rule is not followed legalistically. No principal walks the halls with a ruler in hand, taking measurements. Boys and girls may naturally come in contact during the day. But the rule does prohibit a deliberate physical contact between the sexes, such as hand-holding or an arm around the waist.

An Arizona principal caught a teenage boy and girl kissing at the water fountain one day. "It wasn't a mad passionate embrace," the principal said. "It was a couple of high school students. She was feeling bad and he wanted to show her that he cared. So he kissed her on the cheek." Both teenagers received a thirty-minute detention for violating the "six-inch rule."

Some fundamentalist schools go so far as to dictate no dating at all by students, even on weekends. The belief is that school-age youths should never be in a one-to-one situation with a member of the opposite sex. There's time for that *after* high school, they say.

Bob Jones Academy in South Carolina, which has boarding students in grades one through twelve, is particularly cautious not only with high schoolers but with its college students as well. Hugging, kissing, and even touching are prohibited on campus. Girls don't talk to boys before breakfast. Girls must log in how many hours each day they spend with a boy.

"If a father in California sends his daughter here, we want him to sleep at night and not worry that he will get a call that his daughter is pregnant," principal Ross Penix said.

The campus has a student lounge with dozens of sofas placed around strategically placed lamps. Here, boys and girls can sit and talk but not touch. The philosophy is that a relationship should first develop spiritually, mentally, and emotionally before it develops physically. On this campus, boys and girls smiled, talked, and laughed with one other. But no one was touching.

I was walking with Penix from the junior high school to the chapel service scheduled in the nearby auditorium when a solicitous young man, balding in front, stopped Penix and asked apologetically: "Sir, could I have your permission to walk my girl to the chapel service now?" Penix looked the man over awhile and said, "Okay." The young man backed away, nodding his head and issuing thanks all of the way. When he had left, I asked Penix if that was a father asking permission to escort his young daughter to the chapel service. "No," Penix replied. "He's a senior at the university here and he wants to walk his girlfriend to the chapel service. She's an aide at my school today." That's when I learned that BJU goes beyond no physical contact and a roomful of sofas for dating. The school doesn't even allow male and female students to walk together as a couple at certain times without permission.

The chapel speaker that day was a BJU graduate named Les Ollila, associate pastor of a church in Roseville, Michigan. One minute he had those inside the 7,000-seat auditorium chuckling when he rhetorically commented on BJU's strictness: "What about necking and petting on campus? Well, you've got to be fast!" The next minute he was preaching the importance of living a disciplined life. "Circumstances do not make us what we are; they reveal what we are," he said. "Life is full of restrictions. When you get married, you can't date anymore. You may choose what to do, but you cannot choose the consequences of your decision. That's God's choice."

Ollila told of the time he was preaching to the youth in an independent Baptist church in another state. He said he had felt uncomfortable ever since entering that church and he finally had stopped midway in his talk to say he was overcome by a sense of sin in the room. He went ahead and finished the church talk. After midnight, there was a knock on his door. Ollila said: "It was the pastor of that church, crying, saying he was having sex with three teenage girls in his school." Ollila says he directed the man to immediately leave the ministry and get himself straightened out. Ollila says the pastor blamed pornography for leading him astray. Ollila then warned the Bob Jones students not to let themselves ever get led astray.

At a fundamentalist school in Iowa, students of the opposite sex are not allowed to swim together. "It's like nudity in public," the principal said. "The teenage mind is so aware of the physical. What does the nakedness of a girl do to you? He will look at her and have thoughts that shouldn't be nurtured. What is the difference in a white bikini and wearing underclothes? The same is exposed. It works the other way, too. TV promotes that girls ought to ogle the boys."

Some schools try to avoid sex education but are confronted with it anyway. David Linkswiler is the principal of Cloverdale Christian Academy in Little Rock, Arkansas. He, too, believes sex education should be left to the home. But a few years ago, when he was principal of a Christian school in Florida, a fifth-grade boy knocked on his office door and said he had a question. Sure, said Linkswiler, come on in. The boy sat down, looked Linkswiler in the eye and asked in a straightforward manner: "How do you masturbate?'' Linkswiler said the question unnerved him. He was so unprepared for it that he blinked a couple of times, stuttered around a bit and finally suggested that the boy talk to his dad instead. ''I knew the dad, and I knew he could handle it,'' Linkswiler recalled. The dad called Linkswiler the next day to say he had had a frank discussion with his son about sex.

More recently, Linkswiler had to arrange for a female teacher to talk with a fifth-grade girl who had started having periods. ''We finally had to tell her not to flush her tampon down the commode, that it was jamming it up,'' Linkswiler said. ''But that's about the extent of sex education in this school. I prefer it handled by the home.''

On the secondary level, a few Christian schools are having to confront homosexuality. Larry Roots is a guidance counselor at Jerry Falwell's school in Lynchburg, Virginia. While counseling a troubled fourteen-year-old girl who went to the school, Roots discovered she was a homosexual, had been sexually active since the age of eight, and didn't want to change. Roots is an ordained minister, not a psychologist, so he referred her to professional counselors. In the meantime, Roots said, the Christian school ''had to decide whether to even keep her since Rev. Falwell takes such a strong stand against homosexuality.'' The girl's parents solved the dilemma by transferring her to a public school.

Dr. Paul A. Kienel of the Association of Christian Schools International has written a guide on how parents and Christian schools can work together to avert homosexual tendencies in children. ''Whether we like to talk or think about it or not, homosexuality is weaving itself into the fabric of our society,'' Kienel says. ''Unless we understand the problem and prepare ourselves and our children against the coming 'Gay is Good' campaign, your family or my family could fall victim to this insidious evil.''[2]

Kienel says all eight Bible references to homosexuality condemn it as sinful, unnatural, and a brand of perversion.[3] Parents and teachers, says Kienel, need to discuss the biblical view of homosexuality with children beginning in the upper elementary grades. He says teachers should discuss the problem only in general terms, leaving detailed discussions to parents.

He warns parents, however, to be prepared for two shocks: how much their children already know about homosexuality and how they may al-

---

[2]Paul Kienel, *Love in the Family* (La Habra CA: P. K. Books, 1980) 64.

[3]The eight Bible passages listed by Kienel are Genesis 19:1-11, Leviticus 18:22, Leviticus 20:13, Deuteronomy 23:17, Judges 19:22-25, Romans 1:26-28, 1 Corinthians 6:9-10, and 1 Timothy 1:9-10.

ready be favorably disposed toward it. ''The liberal views of the American media have had a devastating effect on our youth regarding this problem,'' he said. Kienel says children should never be encouraged to assume the opposite sex role:

> Girls should occupy themselves in work and play activities that are characteristically girl roles. Boys should be encouraged to follow after masculine activities. To do otherwise is to force children into the world's current mold of ''unisex'' which is definitely contrary to God's plan. It is important to understand that current unisex hair styles and unisex clothes are more than just a fad. Many of the style-setters of our day are personally preoccupied with a unisex homosexual mentality. We would do well not to be duped into their warped world.[4]

Kienel says children raised in loving, well-disciplined homes with proper role models for parents seldom become homosexuals.

But a lot of kids these days don't have a full complement of role models in the home. They grow up in single-parent households or with their grandparents, thinking that romance is only for the unmarried or the young. The principal of a Christian school in New York considers himself a role model at school for his many students who come from divorced families. He does that by publicly kissing one of the school's teachers—his wife. He doesn't make it a production, but he believes in the occasional public display of affection between spouses. ''If there's a husband-wife team working in a school, they need to serve as an example,'' he said. ''These kids will remember what they see at school. A kiss portrays a good, healthy marriage relationship. Some of these kids have probably never seen a kiss between their mother and father. They think kissing and marriage don't go together.''

Christian schools also seek to employ only proper role models. Several years ago, the coach at a Tennessee school was getting a divorce. The principal called him in and told him if he were willing to work toward a reconciliation, he could stay. The coach chose to resign without a fuss, saying there was no possibility of a reconciliation but also saying he understood the school's antidivorce position.

If many of America's Christian schools show a reticence to teach sex education, virtually none hesitate to teach sex roles. Boys are taught to be the head of the household, with women as the helpmates.

---

[4]Kienel, *Love in the Family*, 66-67.

The A.C.E. curriculum teaches sex roles through units on health. "We feel that sex education is best left up to the parents, but in the health classes we do teach Christian manhood to the boys and Christian womanhood to the girls. We teach virtue and morality," A.C.E.'s Ronald Johnson told me. The company's fundamentalist curriculum in the early levels is written exclusively by women to reflect the maternal attachment children experience early in life. As children turn nine and ten, A.C.E. shifts more to a paternal image by incorporating male curriculum writers.[5]

At Pensacola Christian School, only women are allowed to teach kindergarten through third grade. The school believes in emphasizing the mother role in the early grades.

A big part of the sex-role education is the importance placed on a girl's appearance. Johnson of A.C.E. says it is no accident that the official symbols of feminism are short hair and pants. Women who wear pants are symbolically rebelling against authority, he says, citing Deuteronomy 22:5 which says: "The woman shall not wear that which pertaineth to a man for all that do so are abomination unto the Lord thy God." Johnson elaborates:

> Pants on women reflect an attitude of independence: to move about more freely. This has been an objective since the Garden of Eden. Eve's sin was to know as much as her God and to deny the need for her husband's authority over her. Today, women who wear pants do so in direct opposition to God's authority, reflecting their desire to be equal with men in the sight of others, God notwithstanding![6]

This view that men are the leaders and women are the followers carries over into tangible, and controversial, areas such as teacher pay in Christian schools. At a Christian school in Connecticut, married men received $375 a week and single women received $175 a week. The school principal said that the disparity was designed to attract men to the teaching profession because they offer stability to a school. Of the women, he said, "They aren't suffering. You'll find that they have as much left over at the end of the week as a man with a family to provide for."

I found similar views at schools in North Carolina, Maine, Illinois, and other states. "A woman whose husband makes $35,000 or $40,000 a year doesn't have the same needs as a man trying to provide for his family,"

---

[5]Donald Howard, "American Educational Reform of the '80s," brochure (Lewisville TX: Accelerated Christian Education, Inc., 1982) 30.

[6]Ronald Johnson, *Under Tutors and Governors* (Lewisville TX: Accelerated Christian Education, Inc., 1980) 30.

one principal said. Another commented: "This has nothing to do with equal pay for equal work. We think paying the breadwinner more is biblically based. But I guess this would label me as a male chauvinist pig."

Some Christian school leaders oppose differing pay scales and fear that such policies could embroil Christian schools in a legal quagmire. But the courts historically have been hesitant to become involved in personnel matters at religious schools.

In 1983, teachers at Martinsburg Christian Academy in Martinsburg, West Virginia, were paid a base salary of $7,000 a year. Heads of household were given an additional $500 for spouse and each child. One day, a female teacher asked principal Edward Davis to elevate her to head-of-household status when her husband was laid off work and began drawing unemployment benefits. Since the couple had two children, the head-of-household status meant a difference of $1,500 for the teacher. Davis said no. The teacher quit and later filed a sex discrimination complaint with the federal Equal Employment Opportunity Commission. Davis told of the outcome, pending an appeal: "The EEOC wanted all our records and we said, 'No way, José.' Then the EEOC wanted us to submit to a hearing, but our lawyer said if we even went, we'd be conceding they had jurisdiction over us. So we took the offensive and took the matter to federal court." A federal judge ruled in the school's favor, saying the school is church-related and therefore the government must abide by the principle of separation of church and state.

Davis said the case could cost the school as much as $16,000, but the school is fighting for the principle and not to save the $1,500 the woman would have received. "We feel the Bible does say the husband is the head of the home," Davis said. He cited Ephesians 5:23: "For the husband is the head of the wife, even as Christ is the head of the church."

A similar case reached the U.S. Supreme Court in 1986. The case, known as Ohio Civil Rights Commission v. Dayton Christian Schools, pitted a private school's understanding of scripture against a state law barring sex discrimination in employment.

In January 1979, an elementary school teacher, Mrs. Linda Hoskinson, told the principal of Dayton Christian Schools that she was pregnant and would be giving birth to her first child that summer. Soon thereafter, she received a letter stating that her contract would not be renewed for the following year. The school told her: "We see the importance of the mother in the home during the early years of child growth."

Mrs. Hoskinson, a Southern Baptist who had taught at the school for five years, protested that she had never heard of such a policy, nor was it stated in her contract or in any rule of the school. When school officials learned that Mrs. Hoskinson had gone to an attorney, they rescinded the nonrenewal of her contract on grounds of pregnancy and instead fired her for violating the biblical chain of command. The school system says it acted on its belief—based on Matthew 18:15-17 and other scripture passages—that Christians are prohibited from taking disputes to outside parties. The school pointed out that Mrs. Hoskinson's contract specified the "chain of command" policy for resolving disputes and that she even had written on the contract in her own handwriting: "Obedience to those in authority over you is clearly stated in the Bible. I believe in God's chain of command."

Dayton Christian Schools enrolls 1,800 students on five campuses. The school is funded by parents and local churches and receives no government assistance.

The Ohio Civil Rights Commission declared in 1980 that the school was guilty of sex discrimination, and the commission ordered that Hoskinson be reinstated. Later, the 6th U.S. Circuit Court of Appeals ruled in favor of the school. The appeals court said the Ohio law "in these circumstances was violative of the Free Exercise and Establishment clauses of the First Amendment." In 1986, the U.S. Supreme Court heard oral arguments and ruled that the Civil Rights Commission did have the right to investigate the Dayton Christian Schools' personnel policies.[7] The Supreme Court's decision is considered an important barometer concerning the church-state status of these increasingly numerous and separatist Christian schools.

Sex education in Christian schools, then, is far more than the birds and the bees. It is the teaching of a role in Christian society for the man and a different role for the woman.

---

[7]Ohio Civil Rights Commission v. Dayton Christian Schools, 106 S.Ct. 2718. For background information, see Robert F. Drinan, "The Supreme Court Examines Fundamentalist Christian Schools," *America* (12 April 1986): 306-308; and Vincent Golphin, "Supreme Court to Hear Oral Arguments in Dayton Christian Schools Case," *Christianity Today* (21 March 1986): 56-57.

9

SPORTS
AS A BLESSING
AND A CURSE

We are a people in love with our games. A college quarterback entering the pros earns seven times the salary paid the President of the United States. Millions of Americans spend their weekends glued to one sports event after another on TV. Ask some boys who their heroes are and you'll likely get the names of modern-day athletes.

While recognizing the validity of physical fitness and the merit of competition, Christian schools in general are trying to downplay what they view as a national obsession with sports.

In my tour of Christian schools, I attended a hot-and-humid football practice in Mississippi, applauded good plays during a basketball game in North Carolina, and saw a baseball warmup in California. I watched a coed softball game in Pennsylvania, met the A.C.E. state ping-pong champ in Iowa, and witnessed the organization of a lacrosse team in Rhode Island. Without a doubt, athletics has a distinctiveness at these Christian schools.

The playing field is awash in religious significance. After every home game against a public school, coaches and players at Martinsburg Christian Academy in West Virginia hand out spiritual tracts to members of the opposing teams.

In Tennessee, a Christian school team prays with its opponent after every game. "We went two years and didn't win a football game," the principal said. "It was very easy to be a fine Christian school that everyone looked to as being good losers. But for the last two years we started winning. When you lose, it's easy to pray with them. When you win, it's very difficult. Even our own, they get to liking the winning. We have to keep reminding ourselves that the most important thing is to keep Christ preeminent, and not winning."

At Jerry Falwell's school in Lynchburg, Virginia, they compete against public school teams and hold their own. "We get called 'Jerry's boys' and 'preacher kids.' We play hard. We take the bumps and bruises and taunts," says administrator Glen Schultz. "We tell our kids to play to represent the Lord. If you are losing your temper and complaining about the referees and then go after the game and try to witness to an opposing player, he'll say, 'Hey, what's this?' Sports is an opportunity to show our lifestyle."

The showing of a lifestyle, of course, can be negative as well as positive. Dr. Charles Walker, executive director of the Tennessee Association of Christian Schools, spent twelve years in the public schools as a coach and administrator. During his subsequent years working with Christian schools, Walker said he had seen more unchristian acts during sporting events than he witnessed throughout his public school career. He has seen a Christian school coach lose control of himself at halftime and destroy school property in a rage. He has watched a pastor/coach strike a player from the opposing team with his fist. He has seen a Christian school team leave the gym floor after losing a game and refuse to shake hands with the opposing players.

"I have witnessed so many displays by coaches, fans, and players which were everything but Christian that I have seriously begun to question the feasibility of an athletic program in a Christian school," Walker wrote. "You may be saying, 'It can't be that bad.' Yes it is, and I say that with a sorrowful and heavy heart. More shame, disgrace, and hard feelings have been caused by an athletic event than any other single program sponsored by Christian schools. . . . Unfortunately, athletics has become a curse instead of a blessing for too many Christian schools."[1]

To understand this intriguing perspective on sports, we must return again to the philosophy of Christian education. Christians believe the purpose of life—all of life, including athletics—is to bring honor to Jesus Christ and to emulate Christ by striving to be the total person he demonstrated in Luke 2:52, which says, "And Jesus increased in wisdom and stature, and in favor with God and man." Wisdom is mental development, stature is physical development, favor with God is spiritual development, and favor with man is social development.[2]

Athletics is encouraged because healthy bodies are to be desired in the quest for physical development. As Christian educator D. Bruce Lockerbie puts it: "Sedentary Christians, flabby and puffing for breath, can scarcely be called on as examples of that abundant living promised by Jesus Christ. They can hardly make it up a flight of stairs!"[3]

Lockerbie, the Staley scholar-in-residence at the Stony Brook School on Long Island and a runner himself, says competitive sports must be seen in proper balance with physical exercise and recreation. He adds:

> Every sport satisfies two distinct needs we have as human beings: to test ourselves against ourselves and to compare our efforts with someone else's. We compete to do better than last time, to do better than our opponents. In that respect, there's a built-in danger of yielding to pride of accomplishment and the need to win at any cost. Neither of these two faults, however, needs to dominate an athletic program in a Christian school if coaches instruct their athletes to recognize that they play their games and tax their bodies in worship of God.[4]

The Apostle Paul, in particular, found competitive athletics to be a useful metaphor of the Christian experience. "I have fought the good fight, I have finished the race, I have kept the faith," Paul tells Timothy. Elsewhere,

---

[1]Charles Walker, "Christian Athletics: Blessing or Curse?" *The Administrator* (Normal IL: American Association of Christian Schools, Spring 1982): 1-3.

[2]Ron Ellison, "A Christian Philosophy of Athletics," *The Administrator* (Spring 1982): 4.

[3]D. Bruce Lockerbie, *Who Educates Your Child?* (Grand Rapids MI: Zondervan, 1981) 144.

[4]Ibid., 145.

he tells the Corinthians: "Do you not know that in a race all the runners compete, but only one receives the prize? So run that you may obtain it."[5] Competitiveness, and winning, are seen in a positive light. But Christians frown on making the scoreboard the sole criteria for winning. They believe you have won if you did your best and if you tried to bring glory to God through your actions, no matter what the scoreboard says. Players are instructed to play hard and never quit, to win without boasting, to lose without making excuses, and to accept the decisions of officials without question.

In a section on sports, BJU Press's American history textbook for high school students summarizes the fundamentalist perspective:

> To a degree, there is nothing wrong with an interest in athletics. Since the body is the temple of the Holy Spirit (1 Corinthians 6:19), Christians should stay in shape; athletics is one means of doing so. Like everything else, however, athletic participation and interest should be moderate. The exorbitant salaries paid to professional athletes bear testimony to the unbalanced interest many Americans have in athletics.[6]

Today's professional athletes mostly grew up on the playing fields of America's public schools. High school sports can be a focal point of community pride. It can turn into big business. As a result, public schools in this country generally have impressive gymnasiums and ballfields. Coaches, in fact, usually get more money than classroom teachers.

This is not true at Christian schools. An Iowa church school has a dirt parking lot with a basketball goal precariously hanging on a tilted post. An Arkansas school, sandwiched between two fast-food restaurants on a busy street, until recently had no playground for its elementary children. Principals of Christian schools from Alabama to Arizona have arranged with city officials to use nearby city parks as playgrounds.

A few Christian schools have athletic facilities to rival any public school. Hartford Christian Academy in Connecticut occupies a public school facility closed because of declining enrollment. As a result, the school has a fine gymnasium and a large athletic field and playground. But these facilities in a Christian school are rare.

Paw Creek Christian Academy in Charlotte, North Carolina, built its gymnasium for $250,000 in the mid-1970s with the help of church mem-

---

[5]These sports metaphors are in 2 Timothy 4:7 and 1 Corinthians 9:24.

[6]*United States History for Christian Schools* (Greenville SC: BJU Press, 1982) 459.

ber donations. The Church of God denomination preaches against unnecessary jewelry and other adornments. So the pastor, Joseph Chambers, wrote his congregation this note in the church newsletter: "If unnecessary jewelry has been a problem to you, the best way to solve the problem is by putting it on the altar for the Lord." The appeal brought not only half a dozen diamond rings but also a motorcycle, a guitar, a set of mag wheels and other valuables.

Another novel twist exists at the Christian school sponsored by the charismatic Grace Fellowship Church in Research Triangle Park, North Carolina. At the end of a school day, and with game time just a few hours away, students can convert the carpeted sanctuary of the church into a basketball court. The sanctuary, with its high ceiling, is a school cafeteria on Monday through Friday and then a basketball court after school. Students place the folding chairs used by the Sunday congregation in storage and push aside a portable platform that serves as the preacher's podium. With the chairs and platform absent, it becomes abruptly apparent that the sanctuary has all-purpose carpet bearing the outline of a basketball court, with free throw lanes and all. With the chairs present, you don't notice it. Students carry two portable goals of regulation height to the ends of the court and lock them in place. Then a colorful wall mural above the podium comes down, revealing an electronic scoreboard underneath. Boys bring out the basketballs, the principal gets his coach's whistle, and the pregame warm-up begins. The process takes all of 10 minutes.

Not only do facilities in Christian schools differ, but so do the levels of competition. For every Riverdale Baptist School in Maryland playing in the finals of the national Christian basketball championships, there is a Bible Baptist Christian School in Gulfport, Mississippi, worrying about simply having enough players for its next football game. Rick Carter, who serves in the dual capacity of church pastor and football coach, had just lost his only 200-pound lineman for that day's practice. The boy swallowed a tack while twirling it between his lips during workbook exercises at his A.C.E. study carrel. He was taken to the hospital as a precaution. Carter shook his head in mock frustration, rolled his eyes and said with a chuckle: "He's on a carrot diet to get his weight down. He must be eating everything in sight!"

The difference in philosophy between the fundamentalists and the moderates in the Christian school movement is nowhere more evident than in sports. Whittier Christian High in California is an example of a moderate Christian school. The school has quality athletic facilities, full-time coaches and a successful program. School officials want to see the sports teams in the limelight as winners. "There was a sense that if you sent your children to a Christian school, they were losing out on something," one official said. "But parents today see that we have everything the public schools have, including a good sports program."

The fundamentalist A.C.E. program has a different view. Dr. Ronald E. Johnson warns: "Because of the popularity of sports, many Christian parents believe a strong athletics program is essential for a successful Christian school. Their children who transfer from secular, sports-dominated schools are caught up in the national assumption that a good school is one which has a winning team. . . . But a serious consequence develops when sports are emphasized as the primary focal point for student identification with the school: spiritual growth diminishes and students become shallow, superficial Christians."[7]

Without question, many youths do receive their greatest motivation in school from athletics. They must work hard to excel, but there are immediate rewards for success. From dad's delight when his son makes a catch in the webbing of his first baseball glove to the school's pride when that boy makes the district all-star team, athletic competition is a rare arena where a youngster can simultaneously earn the outward praise of both adults and peers. In sports, there is instant gratification and reward once the buzzer sounds.

Fundamentalists recognize this dilemma and try to praise students for achievements in spiritual, mental, and social activities as well as physical activities. At the annual A.C.E. International Student Convention, which annually attracts more than 5,000 students, athletic competition plays only a small role. For girls, the only athletic contests are ping-pong and volleyball. Boys can compete for awards in basketball, a soccer kick, and various track events. There also is a grueling competition that rewards the boy who can do the most sit-ups in ten minutes, the most push-ups in five minutes and then the most pull-ups in five minutes. The majority of competitions at the student convention, however, are nonathletic. They include competitions in Bible memorization, preaching, music, spelling, poetry reading, photography, sewing, and interpretation for the deaf.

A sizable number of Christian schools offer only intramural competition rather than focus school spirit on the quest to defeat some outside rival. Bob Jones Academy in South Carolina has that philosophy. All students

---

[7]Ronald Johnson, *Under Tutors and Governors* (Lewisville TX: Accelerated Christian Education, Inc., 1980) 64-65.

from junior high on up are divided into eight extracurricular "societies" that provide competition in areas ranging from sports to debating.

Others, such as "Jerry's boys" at Falwell's school, like to compete against public schools. In the process, some get carried away in the interpretation of their victories. A Christian school principal in West Virginia remarked: "This has been the greatest year spiritually for our teams. In every sport this year, we've had a winning season because we've honored God." He makes the sports field sound like a holy-war battlefield.

As the Christian school movement has grown, Christian athletic leagues have been born. But, as in most things new, problems can develop. A fundamentalist school in Florida dropped out of its Christian athletic league because of differing standards of dress and conduct. Cheerleaders from the moderate Christian schools wore the short dresses and did the dance-step routines, and athletes from other Christian schools often had long hair. This fundamentalist school didn't care for that. Now, the school competes against public schools in the area. "We can be a good testimony, and it doesn't cause our kids to wonder about different standards in Christian schools," an official said.

Denominationalism can rear its head, too. Longview Christian Academy in Texas cancelled its scheduled basketball games with another private school after years of competition because school officials suddenly learned that their opponents were Roman Catholic. "We thought they were merely a private school," said San Kiefer, basketball coach at the Baptist-sponsored school. "We played them when we had a broader philosophy. Now we are just going to play Baptist schools."

The headmaster of the Catholic school was appalled. "Ten days before the game, they said they were cancelling our schedule because we had philosophical differences," said the Rev. Bernard Marton of Cisterician Preparatory School in Irving, Texas. "When I heard it I thought, what kind of world are we living in?"

Marton said the surprise cancellation was not his school's first communication with Longview. He said the Christian school earlier had notified Cistercian that it was implementing new rules for cheerleaders' attire and routines performed at its games. "They said cheerleaders must wear skirts no shorter than two inches above ground from a kneeling upright position," Marton said. "They said they may not wear long pants and could not perform mounts, cartwheels, splits or perform cheers with a rock beat."[8]

---

[8] "Baptist School Calls Off Games After Discovering Opponents Are Catholics," wire

The Rev. Jimmy Draper, then-president of the Southern Baptist Convention, said the Longview church was not affiliated with his group, the largest Baptist denomination in the world. "I feel it would be most unfortunate to cancel a basketball schedule on the basis of another school being Catholic," Draper said. "I don't believe that any Southern Baptist school that I know of would take a stand such as this. We obviously have differences with the Catholic church, but I don't see that as being a basis for competitive athletics."[9]

Christians have a penchant for dividing; witness the many denominations and offshoots. In the state of Maine, there are now two Christian athletic leagues. The split came over basketball uniforms for boys. One faction uses the standard uniforms worn by college and pro basketball players today. The other faction believes those uniforms are too scanty and thus requires knee-length shorts, knee-high socks, and shirts with sleeves.

Sports is a male-dominated activity at most Christian schools. Athletic competition by females is either nonexistent or strongly discouraged at fundamentalist schools. A.C.E. warns its schools to beware of becoming ensnared in the women's athletic crusade. The organization says schools that encourage their girls to be athletic champions in strenuous sports unknowingly weaken the entire spiritual atmosphere. This is from A.C.E. Vice President Ronald Johnson: "Girls who perform as athletes or cheerleaders in the presence of males soon lose their inhibitions. They become calloused about immodesty. Their sense of purity is weakened. Boys who watch females during aggressive athletic or cheering activity find their thoughts drifting from interest in the game to interest in the girls. Even the purest boy cannot for long cast his eyes upon physically active girls without experiencing fleeting or lingering thoughts not directly related to the sport taking place."[10]

Girls in Christian schools gravitate to what is available, such as cheerleading. But that is a controversial area, too. Dr. Bruce Jackson, educational director for the American Association of Christian Schools, says the leading of cheers itself is not biblically wrong but some of the cheerleading practices of today are wrong. He advises Christian schools to carefully screen the cheerleading squad, make group devotions a regular part of each

service dispatch in the *Arkansas Gazette*, December 31, 1983, 5.

[9]Ibid.

[10]Johnson, *Under Tutors and Governors*, 69.

practice, insist on modest clothing, avoid dance steps and provocative movements, and have the girls learn appropriate cheers.[11] Of course, what is appropriate to one may not be appropriate to another. Cheerleaders from the Grace Baptist Church School in Portland, Maine, stopped using a yell that included the line "Let's be rowdy!" when a mother from a competing school objected. The principal of the Portland school, Eugene St. Clair, said he didn't see anything wrong with the cheer but he didn't want to offend either.

The former headmaster of Barrington Christian Academy in Barrington, Rhode Island, recalls the time his school formed a cheerleading squad for the first time. The cheerleaders were excited about their first public appearance, at a basketball road game to a neighboring fundamentalist school. "Before the game even started, the principal there ordered our cheerleaders to sit down and not get up because their skirts were too short." The headmaster's jaw tightened as he recounted the story. "They may have been too short. I'll concede that. But he ruined the big day for the girls. If it takes it, the girls can wear space suits when cheering. I told the principal there to just let me know the next time so I can have my space suits ready."

So the debate goes on, not just between public school philosophy and Christian school philosophy but between varying Christian school philosophies.

Fundamentalists draw the parallel of America in the twentieth century to ancient Greece. They contend that what started in ancient Greece as a program to build healthy bodies digressed to a preoccupation with physical ability. Winners of the ancient olympics were heralded as national heroes, much like today's million-dollar sports stars. They say that in ancient Greece, as in America today, athletics began to dominate a larger and larger share of the cultural psyche. Fundamentalists warn that Greece's emphasis on body worship led to that culture's moral decay, and they warn that the same is happening in America today.

---

[11]Bruce Jackson, "Suggestions to Improve Cheerleading for Christian Schools," *The Administrator* (Fall 1982): 5-6.

D

THE HEADACHES:
TROUBLES FACING
THE SCHOOLS

I'm very down on Christian schools. I'm afraid it's a bigoted movement. Christian schools are schools of isolation and separation. They build walls around themselves. There's no question that many Christian schools in the South are for those who didn't want to go to schools with blacks. I'm afraid we in the North are doing it to get away from pot-smoking, long-haired kids.

The Rev. Art Reed
whose church operates a Christian school
in St. Charles, Missouri

10

THE REALITY
OF
RACIST ROOTS

The office secretary remembers the phone conversation well. A woman asked in an urgent whisper: "Do you let *them* in?" The puzzled secretary responded: "Who do you mean, ma'am?" Caller: "The niggers, of course." Secretary: "Why, ma'am, of course we do. We're a Christian school." The caller slammed the phone.

The Christian school movement is perceived by many to be racist. In this case, the frantic mother just happened to call the Paw Creek Christian Academy in Charlotte, North Carolina. At Paw Creek, one of every eight students is black. Had she chosen other Christian schools in the Charlotte area to call, none may have openly shared her bigotry but she certainly would have found some that were racially segregated. The majority of Christian schools in America are either all white or overwhelmingly white. In addition, many Christian schools in the South were founded during the turbulent school integration decades. These factors have combined to foster the image of Christian schools as segregationist academies, feasting on an underlying racism. It is indicative of this public image that a mother, in search of a place that didn't admit black students, would think of calling her local Christian school.

The racial composition of the Christian school movement as a whole is not known. But my observations of the racial composition of the schools I visited, while by no means a scientific random sample, do correspond with observations in the prevailing literature in the field. Roughly a quarter of the Christian schools I visited had an all-white student body. Another half had a minority enrollment accounting for three percent or less of the total student body. This means that three of every four schools had either an all-white or an overwhelmingly white enrollment. The remaining quarter was split between those with a minority enrollment in the four to ten percent range and those with a minority enrollment above ten percent. Overall, the minority enrollment in Christian schools nationwide does not appear to be more than four percent, compared with the national minority-enrollment average of 26.7 percent.[1]

Christian school educators don't like making this a numbers comparison. They point out that their schools appeal to a narrow religious population just as a Jewish rabbinical school serves a narrow Jewish population. Since their schools are based on religious adherence, they contend they cannot recruit mathematical quotas of students equivalent to the larger community.

Some researchers agree it is simplistic to assign motives on the basis of black-white ratios. Professor Virginia Davis Nordin and William Lloyd Turner of the University of Wisconsin found that Christian schools in Kentucky and Wisconsin were more than ninety-five percent white, yet could not automatically be labeled as segregationist academies. They surmised:

---

[1]The U.S. Department of Education gives the racial and ethnic distribution of public school enrollment in 1980 as white, 73.3%; black, 16.1%; Hispanic, 8.0%; Asian or Pacific Island, 1.9%; and American Indian and Alaskan native, 0.8%. A state-by-state listing is available in Ernest L. Boyer, *High School: A Report on Secondary Education in America* (New York: Harper & Row, 1983) 243-44.

The segregated nature of these schools might merely reflect the segregated nature of the sponsoring churches, or it could be a reflection of divergent values in the black and white communities, since respondents indicated that the only blacks who would be permitted to enroll were "those who are willing to abide by our standards."[2]

Harvard researcher Peter Skerry reached a similar conclusion after studying Christian schools in North Carolina:

> At least since the late 1960s, social and religious conservatism has been on the march. To reduce this conservatism—and the Christian schools that have emerged from it—to racism is simply to ignore two decades of social and cultural upheaval.[3]

But many remain skeptical. Southern Baptist theologian Dale Moody contends that fundamentalist schools sprang up in a racist reaction to court-ordered busing and school integration. "They want to educate people in a pre-Civil War atmosphere," he said, "which you might call white supremacist."[4] Clarence Mitchell, a former Washington lobbyist for the NAACP, adds: "Every school that's been started to evade desegregation has called itself Christian. That's not my idea of being Christian."[5]

Leaders of today's Christian school movement say accusing fingers are being pointed at them wrongly. A.C.E.'s Ronald E. Johnson contends the true Christian school movement has never been racist.

"In the Deep South in the '60s, there was a racist movement among private schools, and many called themselves Christian schools," Johnson said. "They took on a Christian name, but they were not Christian schools in the sense that they deliberately taught Christian principles, ethics and scripture. The Christian school movement today has them memorizing scripture and reading from Christian textbooks. It's a total church immer-

---

[2]Virginia Davis Nordin and William Lloyd Turner, "More Than Segregation Academies: The Growing Protestant Fundamentalist Schools," *Phi Delta Kappan* (February 1980): 392.

[3]Peter Skerry, "Christian Schools Versus the IRS," *Public Interest* 61 (Fall 1980): 30-31. Skerry, then a graduate student in sociology at Harvard, spent 17 days visiting Christian schools in North Carolina in 1979.

[4]"Are the New Fundamentalist Schools Racist Havens or Moral Alternatives?" *Phi Delta Kappan* (June 1980): 724.

[5]Skerry, "Christian Schools Versus the IRS," 19.

sion. There's a big difference between what those old white-flight schools were in the Deep South and what Christian schools are today.''[6]

Christian school educator and author D. Bruce Lockerbie of New York said the 1954 Supreme Court decision that overturned the ''separate but equal'' policy revealed a sad societal flaw:

> With this decision a dreadful fact of American life was exposed—the tendency to use religious sanctions as a hedge for bigotry. An old demonic urge in the shape of racial superiority drove some parents to find any means possible to circumvent the laws that would bring white and black children together in the same classrooms. One of these means became the organization of so-called ''Christian schools,'' private academies for white children only, schools in which the word ''Christian'' is nothing more than a code meaning ''NO NIGGERS NEED APPLY.'' . . .
>
> Everywhere school integration has been ordered, whether by redistricting or forced busing—in Boston, Louisville, Richmond, Detroit or Los Angeles—racists have abused the name of Jesus Christ to keep the status quo. Certainly this doesn't imply that every Christian day school founded since 1954 was instituted by bigots, but it does mean that advocates of genuine Christian schools have been too polite for too long. They should have reacted strongly to having their identity stolen by hatemongers. . . .
>
> Irreparable harm has been done to Christian schools in general because racists posing as Christians have had their way.[7]

Those within the Christian school movement worry about this public image of racism. Dr. Gerald B. Carlson of the American Association of Christian Schools concedes that quite a few Christian schools were started because of opposition to school integration or busing. But he said the truly racist ones are almost all gone now. As a case in point, he said a Christian school in Mobile, Alabama, actually dissolved its corporation and reestablished to rid the school of its racist heritage.

Christian schools in the South are fighting this whites-only image, with little success. Trinity Christian School in Opelika, Alabama, had no black

---

[6]A.C.E. will not knowingly engage in an alliance with a school that prohibits or discourages minority students. In fact, A.C.E. prides itself on reaching out to minorities. It provides curriculum for predominately black Christian schools in Detroit, Washington, St. Louis, and other cities. In addition, Catholic sisters in Oregon converted the A.C.E. curriculum to braille for use at Santa Cruz Christian School for the Blind in Green Valley, Arizona. In New Mexico, 60 American Indian students use A.C.E. materials at Bible Baptist Shepherd school in Farmington. Now, A.C.E. is at work translating its curriculum to Spanish for use in church schools in Central and South America.

[7]D. Bruce Lockerbie, *Who Educates Your Child?* (Grand Rapids MI: Zondervan, 1981) 120-121.

students. Principal William Johnson said two blacks applied and were accepted one year, but both changed their minds upon learning they would be the only ones. "We'd love to get past the day of black and white," Johnson said.

Landmark Christian School in Montgomery was another Alabama school without black students. Principal David Pope said the school had three blacks one year but none returned. Two cited financial reasons; one was asked not to come back. "She was a good student. We hated to lose her. In fact, she was going to be a junior varsity cheerleader," Pope said. "But our church preaches against speaking in tongues and all that. Her parents were inviting other kids over after basketball games and talking to them about the charismatic movement. They saw our school as a mission field, and we weren't going to have that."

Pope bemoans the racial stigma often attached to Christian schools, especially in a state like Alabama. "I'd like to see more blacks and whites go to school together," he said. "My Lord died for red, yellow, black, and white. They all are precious in his sight. I'd like to see that microcosm in our schools."

Jerry Falwell's school in Lynchburg, Virginia, is open to blacks but few attend. "We just don't get that many inquiries from blacks," administrator Glen Schultz said.

I visited two Christian schools in Gulfport, Mississippi. Seven of the one hundred students attending Bible Baptist Christian Schools were black. Two of the twenty-five students attending Lighthouse Christian Academy were black. Lighthouse principal Pat Jarvis acknowledged that some Christian schools were started for racist reasons. "A lot of people unfortunately didn't bury their prejudices when they got saved," he said.

The South has a number of integrated Christian schools, but many have only token numbers of blacks. Christian schools with the larger minority enrollments are in the North and Mid-Atlantic states. Riverdale Baptist School in Upper Marlboro, Maryland, has some elementary school classes where two of every three children are black. Faith Christian Academy in Trenton, New Jersey, has a forty percent black enrollment. The Trenton school is sponsored by a predominately white Baptist church. "We try to regard each other as Christians, not as black or white," teacher David Watson said.

Black students going to Christian schools generally like them. In California, a ninth-grade black student said it was strictly his decision to come to El Cajon's Christian High, where he was one of six blacks in a student body of 650. "I like the Christian atmosphere," he told me. "There's no drugs here, and no prejudice."

Why aren't more minority students in Christian schools? The nation's large Hispanic population is easy to account for. Most Hispanics are Catholic, so they go to Catholic schools if they are not in the public schools. The absence of blacks is more complex. First, many blacks simply consider all Christian schools to be white-flight schools. Second, blacks traditionally have had lower income levels and thus less money available for private schooling. Third, we should keep in mind that only in the past couple of decades have blacks gained access to what used to be "the white man's schools." They may not be all that anxious to abandon them.

But there are faint signs of that changing among evangelical blacks.[8] Dr. Melvin G. Hodges started First Christian Academy at his black Baptist church in Baton Rouge, Louisiana, in the late 1970s because he saw a need to do everything differently from the public schools. "You can take it from a black," Hodges told me during a visit to his school. "Christian schools are starting for quality education. It's not white flight or racial prejudice."

Hodges's school, which he calls the largest black Christian school in the nation, has some 500 students through the junior-high years. An extra grade is being added each year until it is a twelve-grade school. Tuition is one thousand dollars a year, with lunch provided. Children buy their own uniforms. The Beka curriculum is used.

Hodges believes the Christian school movement will remain mostly a white phenomenon for another decade. "Black preachers must be shaken from their sleeping slumber and made to realize the importance of a Christian education for the youth," he said. "Most black pastors have not taken an interest in Christian schools. Until they do, black churches won't be starting schools."

In Atlanta, I visited a black mother who teaches her children at home with the A.C.E. curriculum. She opted for a home school after it became apparent that running a Christian school in her black church was too expensive. She, too, doesn't believe the recent explosive growth of Christian

---

[8]A religiously oriented curriculum is cited as the leading reason why both black and white parents in South Los Angeles County place their children in Christian schools. A 1982 dissertation by John Carl Holmes at Pepperdine University showed that a religiously oriented curriculum ranked first among white parents in the reenrollment process, while academics ranked first among black parents who participated in the survey. Holmes reported that the black parents who were surveyed tended to be middle class with two years of college.

schools is related to racism. "It's just that prices are too high for blacks to afford," she said. "It's pure economics. The thing I hear is, no money."

She sent her oldest son, Tony, to an overwhelmingly white Christian school because she was fed up with the values being taught in the public schools. She said Tony once had a teacher who stated that God wasn't real. Then she saw a reading book that called the Noah story a myth. Finally, she read a textbook that said, "Don't you get tired of having your parents tell you what to do?" The chapter ended right there, she said, without saying that children should obey their parents. "That's when I realized they were undermining me as a parent," she said.

Tony has grown up mostly with white friends as a result of his Christian schooling. One day, when Tony was in high school, he asked his mom's opinion on blacks and whites dating. She had been expecting—and dreading—the question because almost all of the girls Tony knew were white. She told him she preferred that he date and eventually marry a black girl, but that it was a decision he would have to make. Tony began dating a white girl.

That would cause a gnashing of teeth at many Christian schools. Several Christian school principals privately told me their only objection to racial integration is the potential it creates for interracial dating. The very thought is anathema to some. For instance, a principal of Marumsco Christian School in Woodbridge, Virginia, expelled a white teenage girl for dating a black boy. The girl sued and, in 1981, won an $18,000 out-of-court settlement from the principal.[9]

This fear of interracial dating may help explain why I found Christian schools to be more integrated in the elementary grades than on the secondary level. In the elementary grades, serious boy-girl relationships do not develop, so schools can have racial integration without the fear of interracial romance.

More troublesome than an occasional dispute over interracial dating, however, is the overall implication stemming from the whiteness of the movement. Here's where the Internal Revenue Service comes in.

The IRS has become the principal player in the myriad of disputes over racial policies in Christian schools. For years, the IRS gave all schools tax-exempt status regardless of admission policies. Tax exemption frees a school from paying federal income taxes and certain payroll taxes. Tax exemption also allows donors to claim income tax deductions for contributions.

---

[9]"The Bright Flight," *Newsweek* (20 April 1981): 68.

In response to a lawsuit filed by black families in Mississippi in the early 1970s, a district court prohibited the IRS from granting tax exemptions to private schools with racially discriminatory policies in Mississippi.[10] The IRS adopted the policy nationwide, requiring every private school desiring to maintain tax-exempt status to publish an annual statement saying it does not racially discriminate.

In 1978, the IRS went a step further by proposing that church-related schools be stripped of their tax-exempt status if they had less than twenty percent minority enrollment and could not prove a good-faith effort to recruit black students. Christian schools stopped the proposal with more than 120,000 letters of protest. The following year, the IRS tried again, proposing that private schools be required to show "affirmative steps" to recruit blacks. This time, the schools persuaded Congress to cut off IRS funding for the proposal.[11]

But in Mississippi, a court order actually requires private schools to show proof of their attempts to recruit minority students and faculty. Constitutional lawyer William Ball is dismayed at the implied guilt the court order imposes on churches. "If blacks do not attend the church's school, let it be remembered that neither do they attend the Amish schools of Pennsylvania or Hasidic schools in Brooklyn," he said. "The district court has now legislated—there is no other word for it—a presumption that church schools are to be considered intentionally discriminatory."[12]

One of those defying the IRS was the tiny Greenwood Christian School, with a total of fourteen students. The school had three black students one year, and another year it had one. The school's first high school graduate was a National Merit Scholar. The third graduate was a National Merit semifinalist. Despite its racial and academic credentials, the Greenwood school refused to comply with the IRS requirement to prove its nondiscriminatory policy. The school's lawyer, John Whitehead, says it is obvious

---

[10]Green v. Connally, 330 F. Supp. 1150 (D.C., 1971).

[11]Skerry's article provides a comprehensive analysis of the IRS battle with Christian schools, and he clearly sides with the Christian schools. For an opposite viewpoint, see David Nevin and Robert E. Bills, *The Schools That Fear Built* (Washington: Acropolis Books, 1976). This book, funded by the Lamar Society, uses the terms "Christian schools" and "segregationist schools" interchangeably.

[12]Beth Spring, "A Christian School Files Suit to Prove It's Not Racist," *Christianity Today* (6 April 1984): 83.

why the IRS picked on Mississippi first. ''Why Mississippi? The IRS isn't stupid. What pops into your mind when you say 'Mississippi'?''[13] The next struggle between the IRS and Christian schools came in the Carolinas. The IRS revoked the tax exemptions of the Goldsboro Christian Schools in Goldsboro, North Carolina, and Bob Jones University in Greenville, South Carolina. Goldsboro does not allow blacks to enroll. Bob Jones does have black students but the school prohibits interracial dating and marriage.

BJU once banned black students because school leaders feared that allowing the races to mix on campus would promote interracial marriage. School President Bob Jones III says: ''Back during the '50s and '60s, the black leaders themselves said this [civil rights] issue will be resolved in the bedroom, not in the courtroom. There was no way we could take them and have that thing pushed here.''[14] In 1971, the school decided to admit black students already married. In 1975, the school decided to admit unmarried black fundamentalists as well. But the ban on interracial dating and marriage remains—much to the IRS's consternation.

BJU defends its ban on interracial marriage with scripture. Emphasis is placed on the chapters in Genesis that tell of the repopulation of the earth following the great flood. The eleventh chapter of Genesis recounts how God gave the people different languages and then deliberately scattered the races across the face of the earth because he did not want them to be united.[15] Bob Jones III contends that God still wants to maintain the separateness of the races. He cites passages in Revelation that say God will unite the people in the end, adding:

---

[13]Tom Minnery, ''Religious Schools Rev Up for New Round with IRS,'' *Christianity Today* (21 November 1980): 50 (1451).

[14]Christopher Connell, ''Bob Jones University: Doing Battle in the Name of Religion and Freedom,'' *Change* (May/June 1983): 40.

[15]Adherents of this theology contend that three races descended from the sons of Noah: Shem, Ham, and Japheth. Genesis 9 and 10 describe the lineage and geographical areas of their descendants. Shem is considered the father of the Jews who stayed in the Middle East. Ham is considered the father of the Negroes who spread into northern Africa. Japheth is considered the father of the Gentiles who spread into Europe. In Genesis 9:25, Noah cursed his grandson Canaan (Ham's son), prophesying that his descendants would become slaves. Through the years, some have pointed to the slavery of the Negro race as fulfilling scripture. Bob Jones believes the prophecy does not apply to the Negro race but to the Canaanites, whom the Israelites put to servitude when they captured the land of Canaan under Joshua's leadership (Judges 1:28-33).

God has divided people religiously, He has divided them geographically, He has divided them racially. But there is coming a day when all of that will cease, and until that day comes, we intend to do our best to keep the lines that God has established.[16]

Jones said that is no obliteration of racial distinctions when blacks and whites go to school together. "They go away like they came," he said. "But the marriage situation does change that."[17]

The Supreme Court, however, wasn't impressed with the theology and voted eight-to-Rehnquist against the two schools in a 1983 decision. Chief Justice Warren Burger wrote for the Court: "There can no longer be any doubt that racial discrimination in education violates deeply and widely accepted views of elementary justice [and] . . . violates a most fundamental national public policy."[18]

That led to some strident language in return. Bob Jones, Jr., chancellor of the school, growled: "We're in a bad fix in America when eight evil old men and one vain and foolish woman can speak a verdict on American liberties."[19] His son, school president Bob Jones III, ordered the flags on campus to half-staff and said: "We're mourning the death of freedom— religious freedom. It's been murdered by the Supreme Court today. I have pity for the heathens who sit on the Supreme Court, pity for their damned souls and their blighted minds."[20]

---

[16]"Bob Jones versus Everybody," *Christianity Today* (19 February 1982): 26. Jones also cites Acts 17:26, which mentions the boundaries of people's habitation. Almost all university-trained biblical scholars dispute Jones's theology. Bruce Waltke, an Old Testament authority at Regent College in Vancouver, British Columbia, said there is no way to correlate the descendants of Shem, Ham, and Japheth with races in a modern anthropological sense. For instance, Waltke says Caucasians can be found in each line: Israelites among the sons of Shem, Egyptians among the sons of Ham, and Greeks among the sons of Japheth.

[17]Ibid.

[18]Bob Jones University v. United States, 461 U.S. 574 (1983) at 592-93. In his dissent, Rehnquist said he agreed with the majority on the substance of the issue, but said Congress had the authority—and had not used it—to deny tax-exempt status to organizations that practice racial discrimination. Rehnquist said the Court should not legislate for Congress. In a related case, the Supreme Court reached a similar decision concerning nonreligious private schools. In Runyon v. McCrary, 427 U.S. 160 (1976), the Court ruled that two private schools in Virginia that advertised for students could not then deny admission to applicants because of race. The Court cited contractual law.

[19]Edward F. Taylor, "Bob Jones University Loses Its Preferred Status," *Change* (July/ August 1983): 21. Chancellor Jones, of course, probably meant to say "seven evil old men" instead of eight since Justice Rehnquist sided with the Christian schools.

[20]Linda Greenhouse, "High Court Bans Tax Exemptions for Schools with Racial Barriers," *New York Times*, 25 May 1983, 22.

In this pluralistic country of ours, we are constantly striving to permit the diversity of religious conviction within the framework of public policy. But sometimes the two come into unavoidable conflict. A century ago, the Mormons practiced plural marriage as part of their religion. Our nation, though, said the public interest must supersede that religious belief, so plural marriage was banned. Today, a similar conflict is at the heart of the controversy over medical care to children whose parents shun modern medicine in favor of faith healing.

Where do you draw the line between public policy and religious conviction? On the racial discrimination issue, the Supreme Court now has drawn that line. A public policy that abhors racial discrimination officially supersedes a religious conviction that adheres to the separation of racial bloodlines.

Christian school advocates warn of what the future may hold if a school can be stripped of its tax-exempt status because it holds a biblical tenet that Washington finds offensive. If minority status for homosexuals becomes the law of the land, could a private school that forbids same-sex dating legitimately be stripped of its tax exemption? If a Christian college refuses to ordain women into the ministry on the basis of religious convictions, would it be stripped of its tax-exempt status for failing to provide educational equality to women?

Keep in mind, the government in this case is not prohibiting a school with a racially discriminatory policy from operating; it is only prohibiting a school practicing discrimination from receiving a tax exemption. Yet Christian school proponents argue that the power to tax is the power to control. Bob Jones III complains that the government is using taxation as an incentive for bringing religious belief into conformity with public policy. He adds: ''There's absolutely no race issue involved in this case. It's a freedom-of-religion case. We believe God made the races as they are. He made black people. He made yellow people. He made white people. We believe God intends for those distinctions to remain. That's not racist.''[21]

But many Americans think there is good reason anyway for the public to suspect racism within the Christian school movement. The very timing is suspicious. There has been a notable tendency for Christian schools to be founded at the same time the local public schools are wrestling with busing and integration plans. A Christian school principal told of four Christian schools starting in Bradenton, Florida, the very year that public

---

[21]Connell, ''Bob Jones University: Doing Battle,'' 40.

school busing started. "I think some of the Christian schools were racist," he declared. "You'd have to be very naive or racist yourself to deny that." Two other Southern cities that have seen a tremendous growth in Christian schooling have been Little Rock and Memphis. Both have a black majority public school enrollment and extensive cross-city busing programs. As a result, I chose those cities to distribute a questionnaire to fifty parents who had placed their children in Christian schools.

Sixteen percent of the responding parents cited either busing or the racial composition of the public schools as one of their top three motives for enrolling their child in a Christian school.[22] Parents cited academic standards as the leading motive, religious instruction second, and school discipline third. Of course, the weakness of any survey is that people may not be truthful. In addition, there could be a racial undertone to parental complaints about academic standards and school discipline. Cognizant of these pitfalls, here are some of the comments made by parents in the survey:

> The Christian approach to things like science and history and even math and spelling is wonderful. The love and understanding from the teachers is exceptional. My child is learning at a faster rate and not only in the usual subjects but in love for God, respect for others, and an overall Christian outlook.

> Our public school is a jungle with very little academic value.

> Public school teachers are prejudice [sic] against black or white depending on the color of the teacher. The teachers are prejudice [sic] against students from the North. They are considered Yankees. They teach these kinds of prejudice to the other students of their own color or region. The above is not found as a rule in a Christian school. I think this is the greatest strength of Christian education.

> Our Christian school gives our children well-balanced instruction in knowing the Lord, the three R's, and in self-discipline.

> We moved in the middle of the school year from one city to another. And I know how mean peers can be, especially to the new kid in the school. I didn't want my son to ride a bus and go to a public school where he'd be teased and unsupervised most of the time.

> My son needed extra reading help. The [Christian school] teacher and him [sic] spend two afternoons after school to catch up. I really feel as if they are taking an interest in him.

---

[22]The response rate was 52%. Virtually all of the respondents were white, said they attended church as a family at least once a week, and had a family income of between $20,000 and $50,000 a year.

Children are not allowed to belittle another classmate, much less use profanity [in the Christian school]. . . . [To go to a public school], my child would have to go twenty miles from home and it is three-fourths black.

Racial motivation is a sensitive, and important, topic to me because I grew up in Little Rock. In fact, my father served for eleven years as its superintendent of schools, presiding over the peaceful integration of the public schools following the 1957 integration crisis. That year, President Eisenhower was forced to send federal troops to the city to overrule a seg-regationist governor and to quell segregationist mobs blocking the entry of nine black students to Central High School.

The Little Rock School Board hired my father in 1961 to integrate the public schools without any more national headlines. I still remember the threats and hate mail he received from the segregationists, but I also re-member the support and encouragement from both blacks and whites in Little Rock. Upon my father's retirement in 1972, Little Rock had achieved a widely integrated school system without riots or chaos.

Today, the school system is more than seventy percent black and rap-idly moving toward all-black—so rapidly that Little Rock went to court to force a merger with the predominately white public school systems ad-joining it. This has driven even more parents to private schools. Christian schools have opened all over the Little Rock metropolitan area. The pastor of one of the newest Christian schools, located in an affluent suburban area, declared: ''This is not an old-line segregationist school. We want blacks in the school.''[23]

They may *want* blacks, but most blacks have neither the desire to place themselves once again in a minority situation nor the money to attend if they did. And few Christian schools offer scholarships in an attempt to overcome financial barriers to enrollment or to overcome the racial stigma that pervades the Christian school movement.

In Memphis, a similar flight by white parents from that city's public schools has occurred in the past two decades. The Southern Baptist Edu-cational Complex was started about the same time that a federal judge or-dered a massive integration plan for the city. ''I'd like to think this school wasn't started for racial reasons,'' the principal told me. ''I'm not sure that's true.'' His school had two blacks in its 720-student body—both on the el-ementary school level.

---

[23]''Baptist Church To Open School,'' *Arkansas Gazette,* 7 June 1984, 2B.

The Briarcrest Baptist School System also just happened to open around the same time the court-ordered desegregation plan was implemented in Memphis. Located in an affluent subdivision, Briarcrest said it worked hard to overcome its segregationist image although it was unable to attract a single black student for a number of years. The pastor said he wrote a dozen black pastors asking for help in recruiting minority students. Only one pastor responded, and he indicated "the timing was bad" because most blacks hold a negative attitude toward private schools. Another black pastor later said, "Most of us in the black community see these schools as manifestations of racism. And when they call it 'mission' or 'ministry,' we cannot help but see it as hypocrisy."[24]

Are these schools a manifestation of racism, or a ministry of religion? The signals are mixed. The Christian school movement is overwhelmingly white, reflecting the structural segregation of the churches themselves. The genesis of many Christian schools also coincides with the migration of black children into previously white public schools. Yet Christian schools have started, too, in communities where no racial overtones exist. In addition, virtually every Christian school in the nation today has adopted a nondiscriminatory racial policy, and roughly three of every four Christian schools have black students enrolled. Of course, these black students—like their white counterparts—have been carefully screened before admittance.

Clearly, the evidence suggests that the *primary* motivation for the *continued existence* of Christian schools is religious and not racial. But that is not to say that all of these schools can evade the charge of racism. To absolve these schools of the appearance of racism, particularly in the South where so many arose at a suspicious time, may require more than the posting of a nondiscriminatory policy and the presence of a few selected black pupils within a sea of white faces. After all, racism need not be overt to be racism. It can be subtle and internal. For that, Christian school educators and parents must look into their own hearts. As a Christian school consultant in Georgia observed: "If Christian schools were raised out of racism, then God forgive them."

[24]David Wilkinson, "2 + 2 = Who?" *Home Missions* (now called *Missions USA*), a publication of the Southern Baptist Convention Home Mission Board (September/October 1979): 16.

11

DISCORD
INSIDE
THE SCHOOLHOUSE

The Christian school movement is showing signs of acquiring the headaches associated with maturity. As its numbers increase, so do the internal difficulties. More and more Christian schools are confronting rebellious students, assertive teachers, angry neighbors, and even litigious parents.

Christian schools may be "God's school system," as one educator put it, but they still must be operated by humans. This necessary human element can lead to doctrinal disputes and school rifts.

Seldom do internal disputes within Christian schools come to the public's attention. Each month, newspapers cover the local school board meeting where all of the public schools' problems are aired. As a private form of education, Christian schools usually are immune from such scrutiny. However, in California, a Christian school rift involving one of the nation's most prominent fundamentalists broke wide open, giving the public a rare glimpse into the inner workings of an established Christian school.[1]

The school is Christian High in El Cajon, founded by the Rev. Tim LaHaye in 1965 as a ministry of Scott Memorial Baptist Church. LaHaye has been the California leader of the Moral Majority. The school, nestled on a lush hillside in what used to be a Catholic girls' school, is the flagship of the Christian Unified School District—a seven-school system in the San Diego area.

Tom Barton, a forty-one-year-old former Marine, was hired in 1980 as Christian High's new principal. His credentials were impressive. He graduated from Texas Christian University, earned a master's degree from Harvard Divinity School, and had taught in the public schools for fourteen years. Saying he was fed up with classroom chaos, cheating, vandalism, and teenage drinking in the public schools, Barton eagerly came aboard the Christian school bandwagon. LaHaye himself interviewed Barton and pronounced him fit for the job. ''My impression of your candidate Tom,'' LaHaye wrote Superintendent Bill Kelly, ''was sign him up. He will turn this place into Christian Hi Boot Camp—just what we need. I sense a balance of discipline, leadership—respect and followership of those in rightful authority.''

Barton was an immediate hit with parents, teachers, and students. He couldn't believe the outpouring of parental involvement. ''In my old public school,'' he said, ''there were some 3,000 students but only twenty or thirty parents would turn up for a PTA meeting. At Christian High, I asked parents if they would help out with typing, carpentry, answering the phones. I had 650 responses out of a total student population of 750.''

But Barton, like most new principals, also made waves early. When students continued parking in an area where the marching band practiced, Barton ordered the deflation of tires on the improperly parked cars. A coed not aware of the policy drove her car home that day and ruined a tire. Barton chose to publicly apologize for his decision.

---

[1]The school rift chronicled here was publicized locally and nationally. Details and quotations come from Ted Vollmer's ''Principal's Firing, Bias Charges Shake Christian High,'' *Los Angeles Times,* 30 April 1981, 1, 6-7; and Kenneth Pierce's ''A Case for Moral Absolutes,'' *Time* (8 June 1981): 55-56.

Then there was politics. Shortly after becoming principal, Barton was bothered when LaHaye told church members how to vote in the 1980 presidential election. Barton also argued against letting the Christian High School band play at an election-eve political rally for Ronald Reagan. "My response to the invitation was that we can't send the band because it was tantamount to campaigning," Barton said. Kelly overruled and the band went in full regalia, but no student was required to play at the rally and the school did not bear any of the expense. Kelly said he decided it was appropriate for the band to play at the rally because Reagan "has been a friend to the Christian school movement." Also, two students wearing their Christian High jackets appeared at a rally for Tom Metzger, a Ku Klux Klan leader running for Congress. The students read a message for the television cameras supporting Metzger's congressional bid "as students in Christian schools."

On the day after the election, Barton met with his staff to discuss how politics should be treated on campus. Kelly learned of the meeting and told LaHaye in a confidential memo that he had warned Barton that "it would be extremely dangerous to engage in any discussion that might seem contrary to the generally understood political position of the institution."

Shortly after the warning, Barton says LaHaye approached him and said, "When we hired you, Tom, we assumed you were one of us. But in recent weeks there has been cause for concern as to where you're coming from. Just where are you coming from politically?"

Barton, a registered Democrat, said he tried to reassure LaHaye that he shared the same conservative philosophy despite his party affiliation and asked if there was any way to prove he was not a political foe. LaHaye quickly responded by sending Barton some John Birch Society materials to study. Attached to one of the magazines was a handwritten note from LaHaye: "Rumor has it that you consider my subscription gift and such magazines as a form of pressure. As I recall, you asked to be informed. Please don't feel pressured on my account if you want to throw it all away, it makes not one bit of difference. I learned a long time ago that you can only help people who want it!—Tim."

A couple of weeks later, LaHaye ordered Barton to dismiss two Catholics working at the school. The pastor openly questioned how Catholics ever were permitted to work at the school in the first place. All teachers at Christian High were required to belong to LaHaye's Scott Memorial Baptist Church. But these two were not regular teachers. One of the Catholics served as a substitute teacher; the other as a volunteer counseling aide. Ironically, the substitute teacher was a graduate of Christian High who said the spiritual guidance she received at the school was so uplifting that she wanted to return to the school upon graduating from LaHaye's Christian Heritage College, located across the street from the high school. Barton said he had never been told he couldn't hire Catholics for such positions.

Around this same time, the school board gave Barton a unanimous vote of confidence. But the day after that action, Superintendent Kelly—who in a matter of weeks was leaving to join a Christian textbook company on the East Coast—wrote a twelve-page memo entitled "Tom Barton in Retrospect." The memo went only to LaHaye and three others. While stating he did not want to be "party to any character assassination," Kelly described Barton as "basically a very insecure man who has developed a habit pattern of bluff and bravado which captivates most people initially. He says the right things and uses all of the right Christian cliches and flag words." Kelly concluded that Barton eventually would have to be fired, but now was not the time since "I feel that there is such a ground swell of negative criticism within the core of the high school faculty that if Tom were fired at this moment, the faculty would make him a martyr and possibly split the school."

Then came a disciplinary problem. Eight students were caught with two six-packs of beer on a chaperoned trip to New York City. Barton handed them lengthy suspensions, but school board members felt he had been too lax and instead moved to expel the students. Threatened with the possibility of a parental lawsuit, the school board backed down.

The following week, LaHaye called a special school board meeting. Barton wasn't invited. LaHaye called the principal a poor leader, a liar, and an individual who lacked emotional control. The board voted ten to one to fire Barton immediately. One board member described the decision to fire Barton as "a long, drawn-out, prayed-over thing." At least five teachers resigned in protest,[2] but there was no schoolwide split.

After the firing, a disgruntled school board member obtained Kelly's secret "Tom Barton in Retrospect" memo and made it public. Kelly, who by then had moved to the East Coast, was chagrined that the memo had been used against Barton and then made public. "I'm a little disgusted and disappointed," he said. "I wanted to walk away from that position with integrity and dignity. At this point, I don't care any more what the people back there think. That whole part of my life is irrelevant."

---

[2]At the end of the school term, 17 teachers at Christian High resigned. Five openly said it was in protest of Barton's firing.

Barton left quietly, and the school board agreed to keep paying his salary and benefits through the end of the school term. But the school board abruptly cut off Barton's salary and benefits in April, saying he had found a job as a substitute teacher in the public schools. Ironically, the action came on the same day a reporter from the *Los Angeles Times* called school officials to inquire about the internal dispute. Barton, believing the board's decision to stop paying him was in retaliation for the *Times* inquiry, called a news conference to break his three-month public silence. Barton took some potshots at LaHaye, author of the book *The Battle for the Mind.* Said Barton: ''The tragedy is that in Tim LaHaye's quest and compulsion to win the battle of the mind, he has begun to lose the battle of the spirit. Shouldn't Christians be concerned with empathy, compassion, and reaching out? Christians should be in the world but not of it, and at Scott Memorial the tendency was to be out of this world completely.''

Barton's successor was Bob Olson, an amiable career educator who had taught in the San Diego public schools for seventeen years before joining the Christian Unified School District. On the very day I arrived to visit Christian High, Olson was fired after two years in the job. ''My firing came as a complete surprise to me. I didn't expect it,'' a slightly embarrassed Olson told me. He said all that he had been told was that the school board wanted ''a different style of leadership.'' The new district superintendent, Dr. Alex Lackey, also resigned. Lackey, the former head of the fine arts department at LaHaye's Christian Heritage College, issued this statement: ''I am thankful for the success that God has showed during my term of administration at Christian Unified Schools. However, I feel it is not God's will for me to return and I have told the board that I will not sign a new contract.''

Both men refused to go into detail. But an anonymous letter to local newspapers from a Christian High teacher blamed the latest blowup on the authoritarian leadership of the Rev. David Jeremiah, who succeeded LaHaye as pastor of Scott Memorial Baptist Church when LaHaye went full time into his Family Life Seminars ministry. The letter said Jeremiah stifled free expression. ''We know that Jeremiah would fire all of us if we wrote letters or signed a petition,'' the teacher wrote. ''We feel the school is worth saving, and we want Alex Lackey back as superintendent and Bob Olson back as principal.''[3]

---

[3]Jane Applegate, ''Internal Politics Discounted in Church School Turmoil,'' *San Diego Union,* 6 April 1983, 1B. Additional news stories on this second controversy involving

In addition, a longtime church member went public to say that Jeremiah dominated the school board and was openly more enthusiastic about building the school's athletic program than academics. Jeremiah declined comment.

When I returned to Olson's office at the end of the school day, he was putting on his coat and starting for his car. The local afternoon paper had just arrived, and his firing was the lead story on page one. At the office door, he turned and said with a sigh: "Well, it happens. The average life of a Christian school principal is less than three years. You ought to find out why."

After visiting Christian schools in thirty states, I believe I know why. Fundamentalist pastors are authoritarian by nature. Functionally, a David Jeremiah in his church is more potent and authoritative than a Pope John Paul II in his. Fundamentalist pastors expect to run their new schools like their churches, and that conflicts with the way career educators are accustomed to operating. This is a natural area of fallout from the infusion of trained educators into what essentially is a religious operation.

During a visit with LaHaye at his El Cajon headquarters, we talked about the controversies that caused the school he founded to be searching for both its third principal and its third superintendent in three years. I asked LaHaye if persons shouldn't expect more harmony at a Christian school. LaHaye responded by saying that public schools have personnel problems, too. He paused and added, "And we Christians aren't infallible."

Besides personnel problems, the Christian school movement is experiencing other internal travails:

Rebellious students. At Riverdale Baptist School in Maryland, four honors students published an underground newspaper they dubbed "The Waste Paper." The publication promised to "reveal gross injustices" at the school. But it never got the opportunity. It had a short life span—one issue. When called on the carpet, the students claimed the three-page photocopied paper was only a prank to prod the administration into starting a long-promised student newspaper. But the Rev. Herbert Fitzpatrick, pastor of Riverdale Baptist Church and director of the school, called the newspaper "satanic" and threatened to strip the students of their class offices and honors. Three of them were senior class officers and two were members of a national Christian honor society. After meeting with their par-

---

Christian High included "Principal of Parochial School Fired," *San Diego Union,* 5 April 1983, 1B; and Steve Petix's "Christian High Principal Is Fired," *The Daily Californian,* 5 April 1983, 1.

ents, Fitzpatrick decided to simply require the four students to publicly apologize at a schoolwide assembly. "Perhaps when we saw the paper, we might have overreacted," Fitzpatrick said later. "But we thought it was rebellion." Nevertheless, two of the troublemakers were expelled from the Christian honor society anyway for writing two scathing poems for an English class. The poems referred to administrators as "twits" and "incompetents." The teacher turned the poems over to the principal, and Fitzpatrick removed the budding poets from the honor society because their behavior was a bad example of Christian leadership.[4]

Militant parents. Parents are beginning to see the Christian school as just another organization to be taken to court if all does not go well. The parents of a fifth-grade girl who was paddled at the Paw Creek Christian Academy in Charlotte, North Carolina, transferred their daughter to a public school and filed a lawsuit seeking more than $200,000 in damages. When the case came to trial in 1981, the parents claimed that two former teachers—one by this time had moved to West Virginia and the other had become a missionary in Australia—caused bruises and lasting psychological damage. The school's attorney argued, "We contend the only damage to the child was caused by all the parents' hoopla. The girl herself says the paddling didn't bother her." A jury sided with the school and refused to award any damages for assault and battery in the corporal punishment case.

Complaining neighbors. As more church buildings that once were empty on weekdays become filled with noisy schoolchildren, neighbors are beginning to frown. It's not just the noise; it's the daily traffic and the building construction that often follow the start of a Christian school. Hundreds of complaining neighbors went to the City Council and forced the First Assembly of God Church in Alexandria, Virginia, to limit its school enrollment to seventy-five students.[5] In Maine, a Baptist church fought with city planners for two years before finally winning approval to build an extension to the church in conjunction with its Christian school. The principal said, "The city says we're not just a church; we're a major developer."

Doctrinal disputes. Sometimes a church school's doctrine conflicts with a parent's doctrine. This happened at Martinsburg Christian Academy,

[4]Leon Wynter, "Student Publication Stirs Fuss at Christian School," *Washington Post,* 22 March 1982, 6B.

[5]Gayle Young, "Church Opens Door to Students," *Washington Post,* 6 October 1982, Virginia section, 6.

sponsored by a Baptist church in West Virginia. "We feel this is a missionary outreach. Baptist doctrine is taught," said principal Edward Davis. "A Church of Christ child got saved at school one day. We sent a note home to his parents that said 'Brian got saved today.' The mother got mad and told us that Brian was not 'saved' until he had been baptized. Well, that's the Church of Christ doctrine. Brian was crying and it was a big scene." Brian was a second grader.

Disciplinary disputes. Quite a few Christian schools limit their school enrollment only to church members. This eliminates the concept of the school as an outreach ministry, but it also eliminates disputes involving outsiders. One year, several students were caught cheating at the Grace Baptist Church School in Portland, Maine. One of the students was the daughter of the pastor of a nearby church. Since the school is directly tied to the church, the principal decided to have the students appear before the church's trustees for disciplinary action. The pastor withdrew his daughter from the school rather than have her submit to disciplining by another church's trustees.

Church motives. Christian school consultant William Hipps of Lawrenceville, Georgia, says a lot of schools have been started for the wrong reasons. "Let's face it," Hipps remarked as we sat in his family den one Sunday afternoon. "A school is a drawing card in affluent, suburban cities. On the average, a school will increase your Sunday School and church membership by twenty-five percent. It means bucks in the offering plate." And another complaint from Hipps: "Pastors feel they can handle the children with young, sweet cherub faces. That's why there are so many Christian schools going up only to the sixth, seventh, and eighth grades. They don't want problems with drugs, pornography, immoral sex. They're not ready to handle that. Well, do we stop ministering at age thirteen or fourteen, or do we go on?"

Parent motives. Christian school leaders decry the trend for parents to turn to their schools purely because of dissatisfaction with the public schools. They want parents to share their philosophy of a distinctive Bible-based curriculum. One principal in Connecticut says the top reason cited by parents wanting to enroll their children in his school is drugs in the public schools. "I do not accept that as a reason to enroll in our school," he said. "That's a byproduct, but not the reason we started this school. I tell them to think of another reason. The other reason is a desire for a Bible-based philosophy." Then there is the Indiana principal who had a parent tell him: "We've tried all kinds of schools and now we're trying yours. If you can't straighten Billy out, the next step is the military academy.'' The principal replied: ''Forget it. We're a school, not a reform agency.''

Christian motives. ''I'm very down on Christian schools,'' said the Rev. Art Reed. The statement caught me by surprise since his church operates a Christian school in St. Charles, Missouri. ''I'm afraid it's a bigoted movement,'' he continued. ''Christian schools are schools of isolation and separation. They build walls around themselves. There's no question that many Christian schools in the South are for those who didn't want to go to school with blacks. I'm afraid we in the North are doing it to get away from pot-smoking, long-haired kids.'' Reed said intent is the key. The intent of his Christian elementary school, he said, is to train youngsters to infiltrate the world and transform it. Without the attitude of wanting to change the prevailing system, Reed said the Christian school movement is simply a method of withdrawing from a troubling society. ''The prevailing attitude is 'we' versus 'them.' That's not the spirit of Jesus Christ, but a spirit of militant judgmental people,'' Reed said. ''If indeed we Christians are on one side and non-Christians are on the other, it's not for us to look at them as a bunch of devils. Our concern needs to be to have a tear in our heart about them. Our motivation needs to be creating not judges, but loving people who will go back into the world. But we treat it like the sheep farmers versus the cattle ranchers, the Hatfields versus the McCoys. It's one of the most subtle forms of bigotry.''

Repressive schools. A strictness that borders on repressiveness could be the dark underside of the Christian school movement. Several pastors and principals across the nation expressed concern that too many fundamentalist schools have atmospheres that stifle individual thought and development. This story, shared by a pastor in the Midwest on promise he not be identified, illustrates the concern. The pastor said he took his seventeen-year-old son to a large Christian academy one summer to look it over and possibly enroll for the fall. School officials pointedly told the boy his long hair and jeans would have to go. After hearing a multitude of other rules and restrictions, the pastor and his son talked it over and agreed the school was overly repressive. With his dad's blessing, the son enrolled elsewhere. In the middle of the school term, the son abruptly asked to be enrolled in the strict Christian school. The good communication link between father and son also seemed to break down at this time. The concerned father didn't understand why until weeks later—after his son had cut his hair, tossed aside his jeans, and started going to the other school. ''My son,'' the pastor said, pausing to have a sip of coffee, ''had been going with a nice girl for some time. I eventually found out he had gotten her pregnant, and they had agreed to an abortion without telling anyone. He was afraid if it got out, he would disgrace me as a pastor.'' He paused again, fumbling the cup in front of him. ''We finally had a heart-to-heart talk. He told me he placed himself in that repressive school as punishment. He said he felt he deserved it.''

Assertive teachers. The larger Christian schools are having to operate more like big business, with staff lawyers and explicit contractual agreements, to protect themselves in the event of a teacher dispute. For instance, many schools are building certain ''lifestyle requirements'' into contracts as a result of a teacher lawsuit in northern California. In June 1982, Rebecca Brown, a junior-high teacher at Baymonte Christian School in Scotts Valley, California, married Leonard Groner, a Jewish botanist. That August, Superintendent Louis Mann asked the woman—now Rebecca Groner—to resign. The superintendent cited the biblical injunction in 2 Corinthians 6:14: ''Be ye not unequally yoked together with unbelievers.'' In 1983, Mrs. Groner filed a $200,000 lawsuit against the Christian school, alleging breach of contract and religious and marital discrimination in violation of fair employment laws.[6] The outcome of the lawsuit will hinge on the question of what takes precedence: a church school's right to hire and fire its faculty on the basis of separation of church and state, or an individual's right to not be discriminated against in employment. Baymonte Christian, of course, contends the school simply is an arm of the church and the court cannot regulate a church's hiring practices. Mrs. Groner contends Baymonte Christian, instead, is first and foremost a school and the court's duty is to prevent discriminatory employment practices in education.

Dr. Paul A. Kienel of the California-based Association of Christian Schools International says the school clearly was in the right to have dismissed Mrs. Groner. ''We must not confuse the Jewish faith with the Jewish people,'' Kienel said. ''We have no negative feelings toward the Jewish people. In fact, they're God's chosen people. But if a Christian marries a person of the Jewish faith, then that person is violating a scriptural principle. To violate that is an affront to the school and to Jesus Christ himself. . . . I think what's happening up in northern California is that they're confusing this scriptural principle with racism. It was very specifically spelled out in the school's bylaws that the faculty is not to be unequally yoked to-

[6]Roberta Green, ''Marriage vs. Teaching Job: Issue of Faith?,'' *The Register* (Santa Ana CA), 13 July 1983, 1, 5B; and additional interview notes provided by Green.

gether with unbelievers. The idea that an evangelical Christian would marry someone who does not acknowledge Jesus Christ [as Lord] is something so rare and unusual that nobody thought of putting it in the contract. I suspect that now everyone will put it in their teacher contracts.''[7]

While Christian schools reject suggestions of discrimination on the basis of color, they readily acknowledge they discriminate on the basis of religion.

The Jewish faith is not the one that rankles fundamentalist Christians the most. Catholicism is. Fundamentalists tend to be strongly anti-Catholic—not against the person, at least theoretically, but against the belief system. Fundamentalists consider Catholicism to be a form of fraudulent Christianity. Check this definition from *The Christian Student Dictionary:*

> *Roman Catholic Church*—A church which claims to be Christian, but recognizes the Pope as supreme and its church tradition as more important than the Bible.[8]

Fundamentalists abhor a variety of Catholic practices and beliefs. They object to the pope's pronouncements being accorded equal status with the Scripture. They object to the practice of infant baptism rather than a baptism based on personal allegiance to Jesus Christ. They object to the sacraments being accorded a mysticism rather than a mere symbolism. They object to the confession of sins through a priest rather than directly to God. They object to the special reverence given to the Virgin Mary that they say is not supported by scripture. They object to the decoration of churches with statues of saints—a form of ''graven images'' to them.

Dennis Goodman, whose wife is an ex-Catholic, confronted these issues at his American Heritage Christian School in Yuma, Arizona. ''Last year the school had two Catholics. We have none this year,'' he said. ''I told a family, 'We aren't trying to change your religion. My concern is for the child.' Why put the child in conflict? We believe in the priesthood of the believer. So she would pray directly to God here at school. Then on Sunday it'd be all different at her Catholic church. I had one girl who wanted

---

[7]Interestingly, Green found that Jewish and Catholic schools in the area have similar, but less stringent, policies. The Hebrew Academy in Westminster does not allow non-Jews, or Jews who are married to non-Jews, to teach in the religion department. Non-Jews, however, are allowed to teach general courses. Catholic schools in the area surveyed by Green have a similar policy.

[8]*The Christian Student Dictionary* (Greenville SC: Bob Jones University Press, 1982) 608.

to put a statue of Mary on her desk. I said no.'' Goodman says the girl stayed in the school and eventually became ''saved.''

Delaware County Christian School near Philadelphia doesn't have any Catholics among its 745 students representing 140 churches. Catholics aren't banned; a school official says they simply wouldn't fit in.

Manhattan Christian Academy in New York City has the distinction of having a majority of its students coming from Catholic backgrounds. Ninety percent of the student body is Spanish-speaking. But the principal, David Whitaker, doesn't consider Catholics in general to be Christians ''although they feel they're Christians.'' However, he believes it possible for a person to become a Christian and still remain a Catholic.

At Bob Jones Academy, prayer requests dot the high school bulletin board. People are asked to pray by name for a young man ''in the charismatic movement'' and for a student's father ''who left his family and has gone into sin.'' Another request on the bulletin board is for:

> Those who will be receiving tracts—that they will read them and trust Christ. Many of these people who receive the tracts are Roman Catholics.

Nonfundamentalist Christian schools don't view Catholics in the same theological light. An English teacher at Christian Life Academy in Baton Rouge, Louisiana, says: ''Our Bible beliefs are basic but not legalistic. We have Catholic and Jewish students as well as a Moslem. We teach acceptance of all denominations, that we are all children of God. On Ash Wednesday, our Catholic kids came with ashes on their heads. We didn't have any complaints. There's a real acceptance of kids who are different. The greatest tool of the devil is causing us to mistrust other denominations.''

The three major Christian textbook publishers all come across as anti-Catholic both historically and present-day.

A history teacher at Grace Heritage School in Research Triangle Park, North Carolina, tells students at the beginning of the year to ignore the anti-Catholic bias in their Beka textbook. For instance, a world history text for sixth graders says Catholic priests converted many Indians in Latin America to Catholicism ''often at the point of a sword'' and quotes a Protestant educator as saying ''the Roman Catholic church has withheld the Bible from the people of Latin America.''[9]

---

[9]*New World History and Geography in Christian Perspective* (Pensacola FL: A Beka Book Publications, 1982) 176-77.

A headline in the opening chapter of BJU Press's history book for eleventh graders is entitled "Catholicism Enslaves Man." The chapter goes on to say:

> The Roman Catholic system ensured the people's intellectual and spiritual ignorance by depriving them of God's infallible Word and placing in their hands instead the traditions of fallible men.
> Without the light of God's Word to guide them, the people were led into the Dark Ages, a time of spiritual error and paganism. The mass replaced the Lord's Supper; church ritual supplanted salvation by grace. Sinful, human priests replaced Christ, the true believer's great High Priest and the only Mediator between God and man (1 Timothy 2:5). By resorting to blackmail, priests used the confessional to control their parishioners. Purgatory took its supposed place beside hell, so that the church could collect money from parishioners by offering a false hope that dead loved ones might be delivered from torment through financial sacrifices.[10]

The anti-Catholic fervor is not restricted to the historical. A twelfth-grade-level A.C.E. workbook teaches students that Jews and Roman Catholics "deny the power of the living God" and so lack "the inner power to live a truly biblical, and therefore a truly free, life."[11] The Christian school movement in this nation represents not only an outward separatism from secularized public schools but also an outward separatism from those who were predecessors in the establishment of private religious schooling. This desire for homogeneous, rather than pluralistic, schools is designed to reduce the potential for discord inside the schoolhouse. Yet Christian schools inevitably find it difficult to become an island within the community, separated from society.

---

[10]*United States History for Christian Schools* (Greenville SC: Bob Jones University Press, 1982) 16.

[11]A.C.E. workbook cited in Kenneth Woodward's "Where God Is the Teacher," *Newsweek* (28 February 1983): 72.

12

THE GOVERNMENT AS THE ENEMY

Eighteen lawmen raided a small Baptist church in the early morning hours, bodily carried out eighty-five praying and singing Christians, and then chained and padlocked the church's front door. Authorities already had thrown the pastor in jail.

Some foreign land? No, it happened in Nebraska. The crime was operating an illegal Christian school in a church basement, in defiance of a law requiring all schools in Nebraska to be state licensed and all teachers to be state certified.

In those predawn hours on 18 October 1982, two philosophies of education violently collided at the fundamentalist Faith Baptist Church in the small town of Louisville, Nebraska. On one side, the state maintained that it controlled all of education and that a school could exist only if state approved. On the other side, the church maintained that licensing its school would be akin to licensing the church itself. To these fundamentalists, a church school is not a separate entity from the church, not an agency of the church, not an arm of the church. Rather, it is the church itself in action.

This battle of philosophies began brewing in 1977 when Faith Baptist Church started an A.C.E. school without state approval. A Nebraska court ordered the school closed, and the U.S. Supreme Court declined to review the case. Nevertheless, the school remained open. In exasperation, a judge finally jailed the pastor for contempt of court and twice ordered the church padlocked.

The padlockings, however, hardly interrupted classes at the school. Within two days of the October 1982 padlocking, the twenty-nine students had resumed their studies in a church bus donated by a sympathetic Kentucky congregation. The lock and chains were removed from the front door on Wednesday for the regularly scheduled prayer meeting and, with church members and visiting fundamentalist preachers vowing not to leave, the judge suspended the padlock order. The illegal school promptly moved back inside the church. With open defiance of the state escalating, lawmen started arresting parents. Seven fathers of children attending the school were arrested the day before Thanksgiving 1983. Their wives fled the state, with children in tow, after warrants were also issued for their arrests.

Through it all, pastor Everett Sileven served as the leader of the resistance forces. Sileven is a Missourian who moved to Nebraska in 1973 to find work and soon became pastor of the small Faith Baptist Church in Louisville. He holds correspondence degrees from a school in Morgantown, Kentucky.[1]

To fundamentalists, Sileven became a symbol of ''Christian persecution'' as he bounced in and out of jail a half dozen times. To others, Sileven became a symbol of lawlessness based on a misguided notion of religious freedom. Nebraska's commissioner of education, Joe E. Lutkeharms, believes Sileven was treated very mildly. ''He simply has defied the law at every turn,'' he said, ''and if you choose to be civilly disobedient, you have to be ready to take what the law requires. He chose to be a national symbol.''[2]

---

[1]David Krajicek, ''Nebraska's Question of Faith,'' *Church & State* (December 1982): 16.

[2]Cindy Currence, ''Sileven v. State of Nebraska: Who Won?'' *Education Week,* 23 May

Other foes contend Sileven has "a martyr complex a mile wide." In 1982, Sileven spat on the steps of the statehouse in Lincoln and asked God to strike dead the legislators who voted against a compromise bill. Another time, Sileven emerged from jail to call on God to stop state officials from interfering with his school either "by converting them, restraining them, removing them, or killing them."[3]

Sileven's harsh rhetoric hampered efforts to settle the issue peaceably. State Senator Chris Beutler says: "You have to understand that at the beginning of the argument we just had this wild man, Sileven, up there ranting and raving and getting himself thrown in jail. It has been like having a Visigoth leading the Christians—Attila the Hun in command. It certainly was not a Martin Luther King up there with dignity articulating some very valid constitutional and moral points. In other words, the case has always been stronger than the man who was leading the cause."[4]

But in the end, Everett Sileven won. Weary of the battle and the negative publicity, the Nebraska legislature agreed in 1984 to waive the state accreditation and teacher certification requirements for private schools. The new law does not require Christian schools to provide *any* information directly to the state. Instead, parents who elect to send their children to a school that is not state approved are required to provide the state with attendance reports, assurances that health and safety codes are met in the school facility, and a statement indicating they are satisfied that teachers in the school are qualified. Some Nebraska officials said with sarcasm that the lions had been thrown to the Christians.

The Nebraska controversy prompted mixed reaction among the Christian school community. A Georgia educator asked rhetorically: "Who would have thought a pastor would be locked up in jail, here in America, for his beliefs on Christian education?" A Connecticut counterpart added: "To padlock a church is in extremely poor taste in America." But others

---

1984, 1, 16-17. Sileven didn't stand alone in Nebraska. Other pastors, such as Carl Godwin of Lincoln, were more diplomatic in their defiance and likely had more impact than Sileven on the eventual compromise that we reached. Despite resolution of the matter, some pastors remained in trouble. Pastor Robert Gelsthorpe of North Platte was fined $19,000 for operating an unapproved school. To get its money, the state at one time started garnisheeing Gelsthorpe's salary and bank account.

[3]Ibid.; and Jeanne Pugh, "Jail Hasn't Altered Pastor's Intent To Run Day School His Way," *St. Petersburg* (FL) *Times,* 7 May 1983, 5.

[4]Currence, "Sileven vs. State of Nebraska," 16-17.

consider it a Christian's duty to cooperate as much as possible with state authorities. ''We sensationalize our opposition,'' said the Rev. Art Reed, whose church sponsors a Christian school in the St. Louis area. ''The enemy is not always godless. There's often a godly person on the other side who agonized about what to do with his Christian brothers who are breaking the law. That's a case where the Christian community finally scratched, kicked, and fought so much that the authority had to step in. I'm afraid we Christians are going to take our freedom and the beautiful blessing we have and bring blight on ourselves.''

Our religious freedom in this nation flows from the First Amendment, which makes two statements about religion. The first, known as the Establishment Clause, says ''Congress shall make no law respecting an establishment of religion.'' Our forefathers did not want the government to support a religion. The second phrase, known as the Free Exercise Clause, adds the words ''or prohibiting the free exercise thereof.'' Our forefathers also did not want the government to frustrate or inhibit the religious experience.

Clashes between church and state through the years have swirled around the delicate balancing of these two clauses. In a sense, we have the secularist's rule of separation, derived from Thomas Jefferson of Virginia, balanced against the believer's rule of freedom, derived from Roger Williams of Rhode Island.

Constitutional historian Mark DeWolfe Howe believes the Supreme Court in recent decades has failed to recognize the complexities of motive that fashioned this policy of separation of church and state. The Supreme Court, Howe writes, has failed to sufficiently recognize that the rule of separation was as much a postulate of faith as it was an axiom of doubt. Howe adds:

> The court, in its role as historian, has erred in disregarding the theological roots of the American principle of separation. The court's tendency [is] to see that principle more as the reflection of a skeptic's doubt than as the expression of a believer's conviction. . . . Men of the 18th century who demanded a constitutional proscription of laws relating to religion did so because of the deep conviction that the realm of spirit lay beyond the reach of government.[5]

---

[5]Mark DeWolfe Howe, *The Garden and the Wilderness* (Chicago: University of Chicago Press, 1965) 15, 17-18.

Ironically, the two most prominent lawyers in the defense of Christian schools take a different stance concerning where church schools fit into this separation of religion and government. As a result, Christian schools do not yet provide a united front.

David Gibbs of Cleveland, Ohio, representing the Christian Law Association which he helped found, defends church schools on the Free Exercise Clause. He argues in court that government has no authority over church schools and that *any* attempt to regulate these schools violates religious freedom.

Former Villanova law professor William Ball of Harrisburg, Pennsylvania, defends church schools on the Establishment Clause. He argues that the plethora of state licensing and certification requirements for church schools fosters "excessive government entanglement" with religion—a phrase the Supreme Court itself coined to help it police the constitutional boundary between church and state.[6]

A few years ago, Ball did something lawyers rarely do. He publicly criticized the David Gibbs and Charles Craze law firm by writing the firm a letter and sending copies to other lawyers handling religious freedom cases. Ball, who has compiled an impressive record of winning religious freedom cases through the years, believes Gibbs and Craze are undoing years of careful establishment of legal precedent by defending Christian schools solely on the Free Exercise Clause, as they did in Nebraska without courtroom success.[7]

Christians, of course, don't base their church-state views solely on the Constitution. They look to the Bible. The cornerstone of Christian thought on the relation of church and state is Jesus' reply to the Pharisees when they tried to trap him on the Roman taxation issue. Jesus asked the Pharisees to bring him a Roman coin. He then asked them whose likeness was on the coin. When the Pharisees answered "Caesar's," Jesus replied: "Render therefore unto Caesar the things which are Caesar's; and unto God the things that are God's."[8]

---

[6]The "excessive government entanglement" phrase was first articulated in Walz v. Tax Commission of the City of New York, 397 U.S. 664 (1970). The following year, the Supreme Court applied a three-part test incorporating the "excessive government entanglement" application in Lemon v. Kurtzman, 403 U.S. 602 (1971).

[7]Tom Minnery, "Does David Gibbs Practice Law as Well as He Preaches Church-State Separation?" *Christianity Today* (10 April 1981): 48-50.

[8]Matthew 22:15-22. Parallel accounts also are found in Mark 12:13-17 and Luke 20:20-26. Since A.D. 6, Rome had imposed a head tax on the population of Judea. It was regarded as a badge of servitude to Rome.

One view in American society today holds that virtually everything is Caesar's—that almost all human activity must take place by permission of government and that education in particular is a prerogative of the state. Another view holds that virtually nothing is Caesar's—that since God supersedes government, the state has no rights in regard to Christian education.

The truth, no doubt, can reside somewhere in between. The individual's right to the free exercise of religion is not an unlimited right. Society has rights, too. Ball considers the dividing line to be the phrase "the common good." He says:

> I realize that some pleas for defiance of government are hard to resist, especially when they are made with high emotion and contain citations to the Bible and the Constitution. A sort of euphoria can take over as one is made to feel that he is in the exact same slot as the early Christians going to face the lions in the arena. Well and good, if we are right. But God gave us reason, and we ought to apply our reasoning powers very solemnly, carefully, and deliberately before we make our decision to defy the state. An important step in the reasoning process is to inquire whether the state's interest is one which is truly for the common good.[9]

Except for a few who make no concessions to the common good, Christian schools typically accept the state as a legitimate overseer in three areas: compulsory attendance laws, a basic core curriculum, and health/safety regulations.

1. Compulsory attendance. If we believe the common good is enhanced by every child having at least a modicum of education, then the state must be given a mechanism for enforcement in private as well as public schools. The state must be allowed to know which children can be found daily in which schools.

2. A basic core curriculum. If we believe that education should train our youth to be productive members of society, then the common good suggests that all children be required to learn the basics necessary to serve in society. The accepted basics are learning to read and write the nation's language, learning the nation's history and form of government, and learning to compute.

3. Health, fire and safety regulations. If we believe it is in the common good to have basic requirements for the protection of children, then the state

---

[9]William Bentley Ball, "Constitutional Protection of Christian Schools" (a publication of the Association of Christian Schools International, 1981) 4-5.

must be given authority to enforce reasonable regulations in private as well as public schools. Christian educators emphasize the word "reasonable."

Beyond these three areas, Christian schools often view state intrusion as an unjustified stranglehold on their religious liberty. As fundamentalists grow more separatist in philosophy, they increasingly clash with a government that has spread its tentacles throughout all of education. Battles have occurred over state licensing, school inspections, program accreditation, teacher certification, textbook selection, employee work conditions, legal structure, affirmative action standards, and the power to review achievement results.

The major battles of the 1970s and 1980s have occurred over state licensing and teacher certification. Fundamentalists say these paperwork technicalities may measure the number of library books or may insure that a teacher has enough credits in a particular field, but they do not measure a school's true assets or a teacher's true abilities. Tim LaHaye tells a story that reveals his contempt for the whole accreditation process: "When we inaugurated our high school, a mother inquired, 'If I send my daughter to your school, will she get an accredited degree?' I countered, 'With whom: God or man?' " LaHaye continued: "She eventually sent her daughter to the public school, where she became pregnant before graduation, married three months before the birth of her child, and divorced at nineteen. So much for her 'accredited' high school diploma."[10]

In state after state, Christian schools have gained new freedoms either in the courtroom or in the legislative chamber.

In Ohio, twelve parents were convicted and fined for sending their children to the unlicensed Tabernacle Christian School in Bradford. In a landmark decision, a unanimous Ohio Supreme Court ruled in 1976 that the state's minimum educational standards code could be interpreted as promoting secular humanism and thus was suffocating the spiritual liberties of the Christian school.[11]

In North Carolina, fundamentalist schools refused to comply with teacher certification and curriculum requirements. The state won a re-

---

[10]Tim LaHaye, *The Battle for the Public Schools* (Old Tappan NJ: Fleming Revell Co., 1983) 249.

[11]*State v. Whisner*, 47 Ohio St. 2d 181 (1976). The Ohio Supreme Court placed heavy emphasis on *Wisconsin v. Yoder*, 406 U.S. 205 (1972), which said a regulation that is neutral on its face may, in its application, unduly burden the free exercise of religion. See James C. Carper's "The Whisner Decision: A Case Study in State Regulation of Christian Day Schools," *Journal of Church and State* 24 (Spring 1982): 281-302.

sounding victory in court, so the fundamentalists turned to the legislature. "We simply don't believe that our church belongs to Caesar. It's not part of his jurisdiction," a pastor declared. "If our religious liberty depends on the grace of government instead of the grace of God, we don't have any religious liberty." Under heavy lobbying, legislators promptly changed the law to take virtually all shackles off of private schools.[12]

In Alaska, successful lobbying by the Alaska Association of Christian Schools led to a law giving freedom from state supervision to church schools. As a result, Christian schools are booming in the state. Anchorage alone has seventeen.[13]

In the state of Washington, a public school superintendent complained to the local prosecutor that the Anacortes Christian School was not state approved and did not have state certified teachers. Rather than prosecute, the elected official let parents sign a statement accepting full responsibility for their children's education.[14]

In North Dakota, the county prosecutor in Minot took pastor Peter Graves to court for sending his children to an unapproved Christian school. The prosecutor was prepared to force Graves's four children to testify against him. But the judge asked the state to find a way to accommodate the family's faith. Charges were dropped when the state superintendent of education testified that the school had a certifiable teacher.[15]

In Maine, a federal judge ruled in 1984 that the state education department had no authority to shut down Christian schools merely because they did not have state licenses.[16] The Grace Baptist Church School in Portland was a party to that lawsuit that also challenged teacher certification requirements. "If God calls me to a ministry, I don't need the state of Maine's approval," school administrator Eugene St. Clair told me during

---

[12]J. Eric Evenson II, "State Regulation of Private Religious Schools in North Carolina—A Model Approach," *Wake Forest Law Review* 16 (June 1980): 405-37. The court decision leading to the legislative change was State v. Columbus Christian Academy, Wake County Superior Court, 5 September 1978, and noted in *U.S. Law Week* (47 LW 2212) on October 3, 1978. The pastor's statement was part of the trial testimony.

[13]Wallace Turner, "Enrollment in Private Schools Is Growing Rapidly in Alaska," *New York Times,* 26 June 1982, 19.

[14]"Prosecutor Decides Against Prosecuting Parents," *The Briefcase,* Christian Law Association newsletter (Cleveland OH, July 1984): 3.

[15]"Children Spared by Victory in North Dakota," *The Briefcase* (March 1984): 1, 3.

[16]Eric C. Wiggin, "Christian Schools in Maine Win Right to Operate," *Christianity Today* (3 February 1984): 58-60.

a visit to the Portland school. "We're called of God the same way our pastor is called. For us, this isn't a job; it's a ministry."

Christian schools also object to the state requiring students to take a basic skills test. Besides the philosophical arguments, the test itself often is found to be objectionable. Objecting to the values implied on a basic skills test, a North Carolina pastor said: "One question on the test says Johnny is selling tickets to a rock concert, and sells so many tickets each day. It asks which day he did best. Our students would say his best day was the day he sold the fewest tickets, because he had no business selling tickets to a rock concert."[17]

Attorney Ball also opposes efforts by the state to review achievement results of Christian schools. He believes "the parent market" will take care of that:

> While I realize that fake and fraudulent schools may be established and that it is quite possible that some private religious schools will do a bad job in the educating of children, I believe . . . parents are not long going to invest money in schools which are worthless. Parents who care enough about their children to enroll them in private schools are, by and large, parents who are keenly interested in their children and willing to sacrifice for them.[18]

But others would rather trust the state than individual parents in so important a matter as education. Edwin Speas, Jr. of the North Carolina attorney general's office is distressed that anyone can establish a school in the name of religion and avoid all state supervision. While discussing the North Carolina court case in his Raleigh office, he told me of a pastor with a tenth-grade education who had started a Christian school in the state. The pastor and his wife were the only teachers. "The man was obviously a racist," Speas said. "He told me there are only two things in his town—gnats and niggers. That's the attitude that led to this school. It illustrates to me the need for some state regulation of these schools."

Baptist minister Bob W. Brown, a former president of the Kentucky State Board of Education, says the state's interests require state regulation of church schools:

> I believe in church-state separation. There are parents, however, who religiously believe in all kinds of weird things. We have not so soon for-

---

[17]Mark Nadler, "A Religious Test: How Free Should Church Schools Be?" *Charlotte* (NC) *Observer*, 19 February 1978, 1B, 4B.

[18]Ball, "Constitutional Protection of Christian Schools," 12.

gotten Jonestown, have we? I will *not* concede that parents and churchmen have the right to force children into inferior schools and provide them with substandard education.[19]

Others argue, however, that if our society has reached the point where parents no longer can be trusted to instinctively do what is best for their children, then perhaps we are too far gone for state-approved education to make much difference.

In Maryland, fundamentalist pastor Richard Offer ventured inside the Anne Arundel County public schools, where five of his children attended. The *Washington Post* reported:

> He could not have been more upset if he had wandered into Sodom or Gomorrah on a Saturday night.
> Shameless young girls were done up like "harlots" in bracelets and heels. Young boys cussed and crushed out cigarettes. Lovestruck couples toured the hallways arm-in-arm. Teachers lectured on evolution and reproductory matters. And in the high school, Offer saw the lockers where dogs had sniffed out dope during a recent drug bust.[20]

Offer pulled his children out of the public schools. After they had missed 112 days of school each, a Maryland judge ordered the pastor to either put his children back in school or face $28,000 in fines. Offer said:

> For twenty-five years I fought, I stole, I lived in sin and I went to jail before I got saved. I didn't have half the trouble with the law I'm having now trying to do what I think is right.
> Education don't deliver a man from doing wrong. If the only people who got in trouble was those that had no education, then I'd fall down on the floor and say stomp on me. What they're trying to force on me is as useless as me giving you a rattlesnake to lay down with and telling you he's gonna be your friend when he's half-hungry.[21]

Offer wasn't about to put his children back in the public schools, but he didn't have the money to pay those fines either. So he opened an A.C.E. school in his own church basement, with two of his older sons as instructors. It's all legal. Although school attendance is required in Maryland, the

---

[19]Bob W. Brown, "Standards Are Needed," *The Education Digest* (October 1980): 23. The reference to Jonestown is to the mass suicide by the followers of the Rev. Jim Jones in Guyana.

[20]Chip Brown, "Sodom and the School Board," *Washington Post,* 8 September 1981, 1B.

[21]Ibid., 4B.

law doesn't specify what kind of school, and a measure passed in 1975 exempts religious schools from state approval.

As public-school forces lose the fight over state licensing and teacher certification, they are striking back in other ways.

In Oregon, education officials suggested at one time that all graduates from "nonstandard" schools be required to take the G.E.D. test before they could be admitted to the state's colleges and universities.[22] This was regardless of the students' scores on the ACT or SAT standardized tests, which normally are the only testing criteria used by institutions of higher education. The G.E.D. is a test commonly given to high school dropouts to determine if they have obtained a knowledge level equivalent to a high school diploma.

In Mississippi, principal Pat Jarvis says graduates of his Lighthouse Christian Academy in Gulfport have been denied entry to some colleges until they take the G.E.D. "It's a slap in the face to these kids," Jarvis said. "We consider ourselves a legitimate school, and they earned a high school diploma from us. These kids consider it an insult."

In Ohio, the Mentor public schools refused to accept transfer credits from a Christian school in Brunswick. The performance of the student was not tested. The decision was based solely on whether the credit hours were earned under the instruction of a teacher certified by the state.[23]

These attacks on the academic legitimacy of Christian schools are irritating to those in the movement. The Christian Law Association wrote in 1984:

> It appears that the public schools are beginning to look at unapproved Christian schools as inferior, rather than simply recognizing that they choose to be different. Public schools which are suffering from years of substandard performance should refrain from looking down their noses at church schools that are producing a superior product in the fledgling stages of infancy.[24]

The move of churches into the weekday education business also has created conflict with federal and state regulatory agencies, municipal governments, and utility companies.

Recent U.S. Supreme Court decisions have provided guidance on the extent of state authority to regulate private education. In 1979, the Court

---

[22]"Church School Graduates Must Take G.E.D.," *The Briefcase* (January 1984): 2.

[23]"Public School Rejects Credits from Church School," *The Briefcase* (January 1984) 3.

[24]Ibid.

ruled that the National Labor Relations Act does not apply to church schools. In 1981, the Court reached a similar conclusion involving federal and state unemployment taxes.[25]

In the state of Washington, the Kings Way Chapel in Everett was confronted by a complaint that the church school was not paying minimum wage to all employees. The Department of Labor and Industry wanted to audit the church-school's records, but the pastor refused permission. He said the church and school were one, and that all payroll was church payroll. The impasse was resolved when the church agreed to write a letter stating that all employees were receiving minimum wage.[26]

In Ohio, the First Enterprise Baptist Church in Cleveland was taken to court for operating a school inside a church building. City building codes are tougher for schools than for churches. To be in compliance, First Enterprise would have had to knock off two floors of its three-story building and would have had to move the entire structure ten feet farther away from adjoining premises. Church leaders argued that their Monday-through-Friday school was an extension of their Sunday school and that church building codes should apply. The complaint against the church school was dismissed in Cleveland Municipal Court.[27]

In New York state, eight Rochester churches that operated Christian schools in their facilities were reclassified to pay higher electric and natural gas rates because they now operated schools. The Rochester Gas & Electric Corp. contends that since the schools fulfill the state's compulsory education requirements, they must pay the business rate. The churches, of course, contend they are a church providing weekday religious instruction, not a mere school.[28]

The nonfundamentalist Christian schools do not see what all of the fuss is about. They do not object to state accreditation and teacher certification. In fact, they desire it because it stamps the school, in the eyes of the par-

[25]National Labor Relations Board v. Catholic Bishop of Chicago, 440 U.S. 490 (1979); and St. Martin Evangelical Lutheran Church v. South Dakota, 451 U.S. 772 (1981). A discussion of state regulation issues is found in Patricia M. Lines, "State Regulation of Private Education," *Phi Delta Kappan* (October 1982): 119-23.

[26]"Department of Labor Says Church School Must Pay Minimum Wage," *The Briefcase* (March 1984): 3.

[27]"Cleveland Church Can Operate Church Educational Ministry," *The Briefcase* (January 1984): 1, 4.

[28]"Higher Utility Rates Threaten Rochester Church Schools," *The CLA Defender,* Christian Law Association magazine (Cleveland OH, September 1981): 6-7.

ents and community, as an academically verified operation. Barrington Christian Academy in Barrington, Rhode Island, is state accredited and proud of it. "I think it's necessary to validate us, that we are Christians in the school business," the headmaster said. "This is one way to demonstrate our academic legitimacy." In Texas, all teachers at Waco Christian School are state certified by choice. "We're more liberal than some of our friends in that regard," principal Fred McNiel said. "I have a professional administrator's certificate from the state, and I don't feel I have compromised my beliefs to do that. We don't have that psychological hangup."

These moderate Christian schools tend to unite with the government in other ways, too. Many accept state money for textbooks. Others participate in the federal government's milk and lunch subsidy programs. Still others benefit from state laws providing public transportation for all private school pupils.

Few Christian schools have gone as far as the Catholic schools, however, in accepting government aid. Catholic schools have been financially feasting on Chapter II of the federal Education Consolidation and Improvement Act of 1981, which funnels roughly forty-eight million dollars in public tax dollars into parochial and other private schools nationwide. As a result, students going to four Roman Catholic schools in Medford, Massachusetts, sit at keyboards of new Apple computers paid for by the American taxpayer. Students going to the public schools in the same town do not have access to computers. The reason is, private schools now are assured "equitable participation" in the use of federal aid-to-education money. In Medford, the Catholic archdiocese decided how public money would be spent. It opted for classroom computers. The Medford public schools decided to use its share of the federal grant to pay teachers and buy office equipment.[29]

Of course, history suggests that federal funds eventually lead to federal strings. So a particular government program may be tempting, but fundamentalist schools say no. James Munro, principal of Calvary Baptist Academy in Normal, Illinois, says his school is eligible but always rejects offers of free textbooks, milk subsidies or hot-lunch programs because government intervention always follows government handouts.

In the midst of all of this haranguing against the government, patriotism remains a remarkably vital element in fundamentalist schools. The

---

[29]Joseph Conn, "Computing a Windfall," *Church & State* (January 1983): 6-8.

Pledge of Allegiance begins each school day. Opening prayers call on God to bless the nation and guide its leaders. A.C.E. provides uniforms in basic red, white, and blue with a flag-studded tie for teachers and pupils.

At Bob Jones Junior High in South Carolina, I slipped into the back of a room where an eighth-grade English class was viewing a 1960s-vintage filmstrip on Francis Scott Key. At the end, as Key watched the bombardment of Fort McHenry in Baltimore and penned the words that became the national anthem, a woman on the film began singing ''The Star-Spangled Banner.'' Without prompting from the teacher, who was in the back of the darkened classroom at the time, these eighth graders jumped to their feet, placed right hand across chest and stood at attention until the final note. When the filmstrip ended, the teacher flipped on the lights and said, ''If your flag doesn't send chills down your spine, it should. After all, the future of this country is in this room.''

Fundamentalists believe that the blessings of America are in direct proportion to the founding of the country on biblical principles. They consider patriotism to a nation that has ''In God We Trust'' on its coins to be a basic, instinctual response.

So we have the outward paradox of some fundamentalist schools teaching patriotism, then turning around and refusing to obey the state. They get a tear in the eye at the sight of the flag, but some then defy those elected to uphold that flag. They revere our past while decrying our present. They teach that the country is never the enemy, but the government sometimes is.

''We wave the flag—the red, white, and blue—as a reminder not of our allegiance to America right or wrong, but to the principles on which America was founded,'' said A.C.E.'s Ronald Johnson.

This strong emphasis on patriotism, combined with contempt for individual laws in states such as Nebraska, could cause a contradiction in the eyes of young children taught from an early age to obey authority.

''It's hard for a child,'' Johnson said, ''to pledge allegiance every morning and sing 'The Star-Spangled Banner' and then have the sheriff roll up and arrest your pastor who hasn't killed anybody, who hasn't burned anything, hasn't aborted anybody. He hasn't done any of these things splashing the headlines. All he's done is try to teach them the Bible, and the law says he's a criminal. That's very confusing to a little child.''

Church schools are in the paradoxical position of loving their country at the same time they, out of religious convictions, may defy its laws. But, as Justice Oliver Wendell Holmes wrote, there is nothing like a paradox to take the scum off the mind.[30]

Yet it is a paradox only superficially. Fundamentalists consider themselves to be in continuity with the Founding Principles, while modern laws are not in accord with the true America. Fundamentalist behavior may be more important as a symbol of protest than as a functional act related to the mundane business of schooling. They often view compromise as a religious defeat, rather than as a political strategem. Thus, the government becomes the enemy while, at the same time, patriotism flourishes.

---

[30]*Holmes-Laski Letters,* vol. 1 (1916-1925), ed. Mark DeWolfe Howe (Cambridge MA: Harvard University Press, 1953) 389.

THE PERSPECTIVE: SEPARATISM AMID PLURALISM

I want to produce young people who can stand up to their peers and say, "No, that's not right" without being obnoxious. If we can make Christian schools strong enough academically but not too narrow, it may very well produce the leaven to reproduce Christian values in our society.

Dr. Walter Barge Sr.
founder, Grace Heritage School
Research Triangle Park, North Carolina

┌─────────┐
│   13   │
└─────────┘

SECEDING
FROM
"SODOM'S SCHOOLS"

To those within the Christian school movement, the roll call of public school woes is almost as familiar as the ABCs.

They cite standardized test scores that are lower than two decades ago.[1] They cite busing as an indicator of the loss of community control. They cite what the National Commission on Excellence in Education called "a

---

[1]Harold Howe II, "What Falling SATs Really Mean," *The Education Digest* (January 1986): 18-21.

rising tide of mediocrity'' in academics.[2] Their belief is that the public schools have had to assume so many roles in recent years that physical education, driver education, special education, and sex education now get more attention than regular education.

But their despair over public education goes deeper, far deeper, than these externals. They are convinced that public schooling does not teach values like it used to, discipline like it used to, or instill old-fashioned morality like it used to.

The portrait they paint is almost unrelenting: chaos in the classroom, loss of authority, an absence of standards, and lack of learning. The rhetoric can get harsh at times. "In fundamentalist Christian schools, you don't have kids beating up teachers, you don't have unwed mothers running around, you don't have kids sassing back. You've got control," declared Charles Craze, a Cleveland attorney who defends fundamentalist schools in court.[3]

Today, we Americans take public schools for granted. But a public school was a unique institution at the time of its development in the early nineteenth century. Until then, all education in this country had come from the home or the church.

The notion of a public school system gradually emerged from differing desires. Thomas Jefferson believed an educated electorate was vital to maintaining the fragile Republic. Preachers wanted everyone to be able to read the Bible. Common laborers yearned for their children to be able to advance beyond their own social status. The young nation wanted incoming foreigners to become Americanized.

If education were to fulfill all of these needs, it would have to be compulsory; if it were to be compulsory, it would have to be free; if it were to be free, it would have to be state supported. Thus arose our public school system.

Right from the start, the Bible was an integral part of the public education process. Early schoolbooks based lessons on scripture without it being viewed as a violation of the First Amendment. Even Horace Mann, who is credited as the person chiefly responsible for secular schools in America, advocated the reading of the Bible in the classroom. Mann op-

---

[2] "A Nation at Risk" (a report by the National Commission on Excellence in Education, released in April 1983).

[3] "Are the New Fundamentalist Schools Racist Havens or Moral Alternatives?" *Phi Delta Kappan* (June 1980): 724.

posed doctrinal instruction in the public schools, but he viewed the Bible as common to all and thus appropriate for the classroom if read without interpretation.[4]

The idea that persons can interpret the Bible for themselves, however, is distinctly Protestant. Catholic leaders protested the reading of the Bible without proper interpretation. They also objected to the uniform use of the Protestant Bible—the King James Version. After losing a battle to obtain direct state aid for its own schools, the Roman Catholic Church began building a separate, parochial system in the United States. Later, the Supreme Court provided a constitutional basis for private and parochial schools by striking down an Oregon law requiring parents to send their children only to public schools.[5]

The bulk of the Protestant community supported public schooling from its inception. After all, as education scholar James Carper observed, it reflected the Protestant belief-value system and was viewed as an integral part of the crusade to establish a Christian America. The current Christian school movement, then, represents the first *widespread* secession from the public schools since the Catholics broke away.[6]

Ironically, the same types of pressures that persuaded the Catholics to establish their own schools more than a century ago are behind today's Christian school boom. If Catholics shied away from public schooling because it was too Protestant, fundamentalists are seceding because they find it too secular.

''We had a running romance with public education for over a hundred years, but educrats have betrayed the American people,'' states the Rev. Tim LaHaye, a fundamentalist opinion maker who started a Christian school in the San Diego area two decades ago. ''Christian schools are booming right now because of the total secularization of public education. Ever since prayer and the Bible were expelled from public education, they have expelled morality under the false guise that morality is based on religion. But morality is inherent in the daily stream of civilization.''

---

[4]Richard Dierenfield, *Religion in American Public Schools* (Washington: Public Affairs Press, 1962). Also see Robert T. Handy, *A Christian America: Protestant Hopes and Historical Realities,* 2nd ed. (New York: Oxford University Press, 1984); and Robert Michaelsen's *Piety in the Public Schools* (New York: The Macmillan Co., 1970).

[5]Pierce v. Society of Sisters, 268 U.S. 510 (1925).

[6]James C. Carper, ''The Christian Day School Movement,'' *The Educational Forum* (Winter 1983): 135-49.

In the public mind, the Supreme Court is responsible for the seculari-zation of the public schools. In 1962, the Court forbade the recitation of a state-composed prayer in the public schools of New York. A year later, the Court prohibited state-required Bible reading and recitation of the Lord's Prayer in the public schools of Pennsylvania.[7] Although a quarter of a cen-tury now has passed, the rulings never have been accepted by fundamen-talist Christians.

We must go back to 1951. That year, the New York State Board of Regents proposed a nondenominational, twenty-two word prayer that went: "Almighty God, we acknowledge our dependence upon Thee, and we beg Thy blessings upon us, our parents, our teachers and our country."[8] Each local school district was free to adopt or disregard the model prayer, and an estimated ninety percent of the school districts in the state chose to dis-regard it.[9]

In 1958, five parents with children in the schools of New Hyde Park, Long Island, asked a New York court to end the use of the Regents' Prayer. One of the parents was an unbeliever, another a Unitarian, another a mem-ber of the Ethical Culture Society, and two were Jewish. The court refused to ban the prayer, but did outline provisions to safeguard children and par-ents who objected to its use. This decision was upheld twice on appeal to higher courts.

The case finally reached the Supreme Court in 1962, where arguments were heard in April and the landmark decision was handed down twelve weeks later. On that dramatic day, a ceremony honoring Justice Hugo Black opened the proceedings of the Court. Chief Justice Earl Warren and So-licitor General Archibald Cox offered tribute to Black for his twenty-five years on the Court. Then, as historian Paul Blanshard recorded the event, "Justice Black leaned forward a little, shuffled a thick sheaf of papers, and in his clear dry Alabama accent pronounced the words that went further toward the complete disestablishment of religion than any previous pro-nouncement in American history."[10]

---

[7]The school-prayer ruling was Engel v. Vitale, 370 U.S. 421 (1962). The Bible-reading ruling was Abington School District v. Schempp, 374 U.S. 203 (1963), decided in a joint decision with Murray v. Curlett. Murray dealt with nonstatutory rules in which Baltimore school officials mandated morning Bible reading and prayer. The Baltimore suit was brought by Madalyn Murray (O'Hair) on behalf of her son, Bill.

[8]Engel v. Vitale, 370 U.S. 421 (1962) at 422.

[9]Leo Pfeffer, *Church, State, and Freedom* (Boston: Beacon Press, 1953) 64.

[10]Paul Blanshard, *Religion and the Schools: The Great Controversy* (Boston: Beacon Press, 1963) 41.

Justice Black said there was no doubt that the New York prayer asking for God's blessing was a religious activity that breached the constitutional wall between church and state. Noting that the decision might be construed by some as hostility toward religion, Black took a moment to affirm his personal faith in the power of religion, adding:

> It is neither sacrilegious nor antireligious to say that each separate government in this country should stay out of the business of writing or sanctioning official prayers and leave that purely religious function to the people themselves and to those the people choose to look for religious guidance.[11]

One year later, the Supreme Court struck down Pennsylvania's Bible-reading and Lord's Prayer exercises in the public schools. The state had required the reading of ten verses from the Bible, without comment, at the beginning of each school day. The state also had required that the Lord's Prayer be recited in the opening exercises. In 1958, a Unitarian family challenged these religious exercises. A federal court declared the mandatory exercises to be unconstitutional. The state revised the law to allow those children not wanting to participate to be excused, but the federal court again held the ceremonies to be unconstitutional. The Supreme Court agreed, with a Protestant writing the majority opinion and members of the Catholic church and the Jewish faith writing concurring opinions.[12]

The lone dissenter in both landmark cases was Justice Potter Stewart. In a strong dissent in the Regents' Prayer case, Justice Stewart retorted that the Court had overinterpreted the First Amendment clause prohibiting the establishment of religion. He cited the use of the motto "In God We Trust" on the nation's coins and said, "We are a religious people whose institutions presuppose a Supreme Being."[13]

Justice Stewart was not the first to make that point. In 1892, the Supreme Court determined that America had been a Christian nation from its

---

[11]Engel v. Vitale, 370 U.S. 421 (1962) at 435.

[12]Robert Leight, "Prayer and Bible Reading in America's Public Schools: Historical Background" (undated paper written for The Horace Mann League). Justice Tom Clark, a Presbyterian, wrote the majority opinion in Abington v. Schempp. Concurring opinions were written by Justice Arthur Goldberg, who is Jewish, and Justice William Brennan, a Roman Catholic.

[13]Engel v. Vitale, 370 U.S. 421 (1962) at 445. Ironically, Justice Stewart's statement that "we are a religious people whose institutions presuppose a Supreme Being" repeated word for word a statement written ten years earlier in Zorach v. Clausen, 343 U.S. 306 (1952) at 312-13, by Justice William O. Douglas. In the Engel case, however, Douglas concurred with the majority opinion.

earliest days. The nineteenth-century Court ruling, delivered by Justice Josiah Brewer, was a study of the historical and legal evidence for America's Christian heritage. After reviewing hundreds of court cases, state constitutions, and historical documents, the Court said:

> There is a universal language pervading them all, having one meaning; they affirm and reaffirm that this is a religious nation. These are not individual sayings, declarations of private individuals: they are organic utterances; they speak the language of the entire people. . . . This is a Christian nation.[14]

Was the United States established as a Christian nation? Both sides can make a case. The Mayflower Compact says the Pilgrims' voyage was undertaken in part "for ye glorie of God and advancemente of ye Christian faith." At the time of the drafting of the Constitution, nine of the thirteen colonies had established churches. The Founding Fathers, however, made no reference to Christianity or to the Bible in either the Declaration of Independence or the Constitution.

This question is important because fundamentalists believe this land was formed as a Christian nation, and they strive to return the land to that status. So when the symbols of the faith—prayer and the Bible—are banned from the public-school classroom, they see it as a nation abandoning its religious roots.

The migration from public schools to Christian schools began in earnest after these Court rulings and, of course, the school desegregation rulings in the South. Meanwhile, the public schools have gone through some troubling years.

Many of the teachers and administrators in Christian schools today were in the public schools yesterday. Horror stories abound. Illinois's James Munro says he should have been called a policeman instead of a teacher because he spent so much time breaking up fights in the hallways. California's Bob Olson got in trouble when he refused to take his homeroom class to a student play where guys walked across stage holding women's bras and making jokes. Arkansas's Fran Fulghum says she was slapped twice by students while teaching in the Houston public schools. North Carolina's Juanita Chambers became concerned when her daughters raced home daily from the bus stop to use the bathroom. "They said they were afraid to go to the bathrooms at school because of extortions and threats," she said.

---

[14]Church of the Holy Trinity v. the United States, 143 U.S. 457 (1892) at 471.

Arizona's Dennis Goodman drives by a public school bus stop each morning on the way to his Christian school. "I see young ladies of high school age in short shorts and halter tops. Young men at 7:30 in the morning are drinking beer," he said. "My brother was a public school administrator. He says the teacher's lounge smelled more of marijuana than the boy's room. We can't afford to put our children into that situation."

Another lament is that America no longer has public schools, but government schools. Fred McNiel, a former public school teacher turned Christian school principal in Texas, says local citizens somehow must wrest control of their schools from the government octopus. "If you give people responsibility, you must give them authority. Public school teachers have lost their authority," McNiel said. "Today you can't keep students after school as punishment because they have to ride the bus home. You can't keep them out of P.E. because that's now as important as reading and writing. You can't leave them out of the group because that's embarrassing to them. You can't make them write sentences over and over because that's demeaning and a waste of time. You certainly can't spank. I did that once, and a momma said she was going to come up and whip me."

But, worst of all, the Christian school community believes public education has lost its moral moorings.

"The Bible is very plain," said Memphis's Paul Young. "It says you can't be lukewarm. You are either hot or cold. The scripture says you are either for me or against me. You can't be spiritually neutral. And that's the position of the public schools. They don't teach absolutes. To me, that will be—and is—the downfall of the public schools. When I was in the public schools, even though it was not structured on the word of the Bible, the philosophy of the scriptures was there. There was a moral standard. For instance, teachers didn't drink beer in public. Now I noticed in the paper the other day that a school board allowed an unmarried teacher who is pregnant to keep her job. What does that teach our children?"

Virginia's John Caltagirone recalls the time he witnessed to a troubled girl during his days as a public school teacher. "I told her, 'You've tried sex, dope, running away from home. You need Jesus Christ.' The next day, the mother called and demanded that I be fired because of separation of church and state."

Californian Bob Olson has a similar story. He put a manger scene on a bulletin board at Christmas one year. His elementary school principal told him to replace it with one on winter holidays. Easter was treated as the explosion of springtime. "Finally I said, 'This isn't right!' Christmas is

Christ's birthday. Easter is the Resurrection.'' Bob Olson quit the public schools.

In the push to have a public school system free of religious entanglement, many Christians believe the nation has created, at best, a school system that has no values orientation and, at worst, one in which biblical values are scorned.

The American Association of Christian Schools warns that secular education ''ignores the fact that all truth is God's truth.'' In a pamphlet for Christian parents whose children attend public schools, AACS writes:

> You are leaving one big area of his life to the training of unbelievers who have an atheistic philosophy. Of course, we are talking about the public schools. . . . Your child spends day after day, hour after hour in the influence of an educational institution which is, for the most part, godless and atheistic in its concept of religion; and the influence of your church in the short hours that your child spends in church or in Sunday school is dwarfed by the many hours he spends weekly in the classroom under the teaching of those who do not know Christ and could care less about your child's interpretation of life or how he got here.[15]

The comparison often is with Sodom, the Old Testament city that God destroyed because its people were so wicked. One illustration in a Christian school recruitment manual shows a yellow school bus with ''Sodom and Gomorrah Consolidated School'' emblazoned on the side. A pastor's letter, outlining the dangers of sending children to public schools, says Christian parents might as well be awakening their children each morning and saying, ''Come on, kids, time to go to Sodom and Gomorrah. But remember, don't do the things they are doing.''[16]

Others compare the public schools to Egypt, where God's chosen people were slaves to the pharoahs. The principal of a fundamentalist school in Maine told me: ''We believe it is wrong to send your child to a public school. God says we are not to go down to Egypt. If a Christian parent puts a child in a humanistic school, it's wrong.''

So, be it called Sodom or Gomorrah or Egypt, public education certainly has a credibility problem with conservative Christians.

This is the story of a New York City teenager named Miguel. His parents sent him to a Christian school solely because they were worried about

---

[15]A. C. Janney, ''Who Me?'' (an undated brochure published by the American Association of Christian Schools) 1.

[16]''Facts about Accelerated Christian Education'' (an A.C.E. brochure issued in 1979) 26-27.

his lack of learning and hoped the highly structured fundamentalist school could do something. School principal David Whitaker said the fifteen-year-old tested at a second-grade level. "All that the teachers in the public schools in New York are doing is babysitting," Whitaker said. The A.C.E. school started Miguel in second-grade books. A year later, he had progressed to fourth-grade material. Whitaker figured Miguel would be able to receive a vocational diploma with several more years of catch-up work.

David Watson, principal of Faith Christian Academy in Trenton, New Jersey, says half of his parents really desire a Christian education for their children but the other half just want to escape the public schools. "In this whole area of Jersey, drug use is down to the elementary grades. A lot of parents are concerned," he said.

Fred McNiel, principal of Waco Christian School in Texas, says public schools have become too big and impersonal. "In a small school," he says, "everyone can be somebody. When you start having 1,000 on one campus, you depersonalize. When teachers and the principal don't know every kid by name, then kids can get away with things." McNiel's school in Waco has 367 students, and he knows each of them by name.

A growing number of parents are defecting to Christian schools, motivated not so much by religious beliefs as by a conviction that the public schools have betrayed their children academically, socially, or morally.

Not all Christians have forsaken the public schools. Many are clinging to the public schools as a symbol of pluralistic America and because they believe Christians should not withdraw their influence from that pluralism. Jack Simonds, principal of a Christian school in North Carolina, said: "God wants Christians in the public schools. He does want to shine a light in there because he's a God of love and mercy. Even in Sodom, God kept a remnant of his people there. We have a church member who's an English teacher in the public schools. We'd love to have him here, but he feels his calling is in the public schools."

Christians who teach in the public schools say they are religiously boxed in by court rulings on separation of church and state, but they seek to persevere nevertheless within the guidelines. Jeff and Carol Howard, speech therapists for public schools around Sacramento, California, describe the paranoia climate that Christian teachers labor in: "Anything done in school that smacks of religious overtone is hush-hush. If a child shares a religious involvement that he or she had over the weekend, the child is silenced in favor of little Johnny who attended a football game and wants to talk about it." Mark Hennebach, a junior high teacher in a poor section of Chicago, has led more than twenty students to faith in Jesus Christ. "I don't try to evangelize kids during class hours,'' he said. ''But I will call parents of my most troublesome students and say, 'Your child reminds me a lot of myself when I was that age—always lying and getting into trouble. I'd like to keep your child after school for one hour and tell him about Jesus Christ.' Mothers will say, 'How many days would you like to keep him?''' [17]

Barbara Hampton has two daughters in a public school in Wooster, Ohio. She's made it a point to serve as a volunteer teacher's aide. She argues for Christian parents to get involved in their public schools, adding:

> If the public school is a slice of the world, then it is a slice of that in which he commanded us to be salt and light. . . .
> Make no mistake: it is a battlefield that our youngsters go off to every day. Dirty words are scrawled on bathroom walls. Deskmates swear. Fights break out on the playground. A few boast of real or imagined sexual exploits. Many have as their constant frame of reference those TV shows our children are not allowed to watch. And most important, God is not acknowledged as the Lord of learning. Our children need to know that we care how they live in such an atmosphere, for they are the vulnerable frontline soldiers in the battle of world views. [18]

Many Christians are sticking with the public schools for just this reason. But others consider this a form of societal suicide. Why, they ask, should children be made the frontline soldiers in the battle of world views?

''It's ludicrous to think our children are going to be change-agents,'' Dr. Gerald Carlson of the American Association of Christian Schools said. ''I think it's an ignorance that people have of what the public schools have become. They are no longer these benign educational institutions. Public education has been in the hands of people who have sought to amend, and have been very effective in causing, social change in America.''

Adds Dr. Paul Kienel of the Association of Christian Schools International: ''To send our children out to the public schools to save the public schools just doesn't make any sense. They're not prepared to do combat with a teacher who has a master's degree. Students are there to learn, not to teach. They are there to be influenced, not to influence.''

A.C.E. has put together a film that addresses these concerns. The film, shown in churches throughout the land, starts with daughter Mary casually

---

[17]Daniel Pawley, ''Can God Still Be Found in Any Public Schools?'' *Christianity Today* (3 September 1982): 63, 66.

[18]Barbara Hampton, ''Why Some Parents Go to School with the Kids,'' *Christianity Today* (3 September 1982): 24.

telling her parents at the dinner table that her teacher was late to school that day because her live-in boyfriend had failed to set the alarm. The dad wrinkles his brow, starts to say something but halts, then turns to son John and asks if he had a good day at school. John gets excited as he relates how a student backed down a teacher in class that day. The father wrinkles his brow again. Later that evening, after the children are in bed, he tells his wife that he's concerned about the values the children are learning at school. "It's not the exposure; it's the acceptance that bothers me," the father says. Mary had spoken matter-of-factly about her teacher living with her boyfriend, and John had spoken admiringly of the boy who backed down the teacher. The father proceeds to contact his pastor and start the ball rolling toward the establishment of a Christian school in his church.

It's only a film. But the drama enacted in it must be believable to many since the ending scenario—the establishment of a Christian school—represents what is happening in city after city across this country.

14

ACADEMICS
AND
ABSOLUTE TRUTH

A catchy phrase often heard in Christian schools goes like this: "Public schools teach how to make a living; we teach how to live."

The phrase oversimplifies educational choices by portraying a dichotomy without shades of gray—in this case, vocationalism versus values. Yet it illustrates how Christian schools like to pride themselves on being the antithesis of contemporary American education. In many ways, they *are* opposites. While public schools try to foster an open-mindedness toward differing lifestyles and beliefs, Christian schools teach absolutes in living. While public schools must respond to federal regulations and state allocations and teacher certifications, Christian schools seek to answer to no one but the sponsoring church or parent group. While public schools must negotiate with teachers who have joined unions, Christian schools have teachers who consider their work as much a ministry as a job. While public schools place the burden of education on the teacher, Christian schools place that burden on the student. While public schools emphasize the value of asking questions, Christian schools emphasize the value of learning answers.

These are broad generalizations, to be sure. But academics in Christian schools flow from a distinctly different conceptual framework. I found the following five premises to be underlying principles that serve as the basis for education in these born-again schools.

An absolute Truth exists and can be known. The Christian school movement rests upon this basic premise. Truth is based on the Bible and its authority over faith and practice. In laying claim to absolute Truth, born-again Christians claim exclusivity—yet an exclusivity, they say, available to anyone who reaches out in faith and accepts it. That's why born-again Christians emphasize evangelism so much. They want others to discover Truth. From their perspective, then, it's not at all arrogant for an Arizona principal to say "We have the Lord on our side" or for an association leader to casually refer to the Christian school movement as "God's school system."

All of education must be based on this Truth. If one believes in absolute Truth, this premise naturally flows. Christian schools treat education as more than reading, writing, and arithmetic. Students do learn to read, but by reading books that are designed to strengthen their faith. Students do learn to write, but by writing essays on moral topics. Students do learn numbers, but in the context of God being the creator of numerical order. God is the center around which all school lessons revolve. The principal at Christian High in El Cajon, California, put it this way: "The distinctiveness of Christian High School is that it is Christian. Our guidelines aren't just our views; they are God's standards. We teach it's wrong to steal. 'Well, that's your view,' some say. 'No,' we tell them, 'that is God's view.' When we teach algebra, we don't teach God all the time. But we do teach that God is a God of order. Two plus two equals four. That's an absolute. Just as a number system has order, God has order. In history, we say nothing happens without God's permission. History is dictated by God."

Education involves learning Truth, not seaching for it. Because education is viewed as having absolute Truth as its foundation, the task of education is to impart this Truth to all who will hear. Serious intellectual inquiry seldom is emphasized in these schools. Since the fundamentalist worldview is dichotomous—good or evil, right or wrong, saved or unsaved—students are not encouraged to struggle philosophically or to debate moral dilemmas. Why should they? No search is considered necessary. The Truth, after all, is theirs for the asking.

Since no search is needed, education is authority centered. The key pedagogical approaches in Christian schools are reading and lecturing. Both are authority centered—one in the textbook, the other in the teacher. In the teacherless schools, workbooks serve as the constant authority. In the traditional classrooms, teachers serve as the controlling authority. Christian school educators prefer a set course of curriculum with little or no deviation, and they prefer authority-dominated classrooms rather than student-centered discussions. They believe the teacher and the textbooks can best impart Truth. They believe students can go astray if allowed to search for truth on their own.

The motive for learning is to bring glory to God. Christian schools believe in worshipping the Lord above learning. Learning is viewed as a means to an end, as a process to worship the Lord, not as something inherently good or satisfying in itself. As an English teacher at Bob Jones Academy told her eighth-grade class at the beginning of a grammar lesson: "Good grammar is a good testimony." All of learning within these schools has a vocational purpose—the vocation being Christian service, either full-time as in the pastorate or part-time as a church worker. A Christian school education is geared to producing learned and dedicated Christians. Penmanship lessons for third and fourth graders at an Arkansas school incorporated the writing of verses from Ephesians and Proverbs. A sixth-grade spelling quiz contained words such as "jealous" and "knew." The teacher put them in context by creating these impromptu sentences: "God is a jealous God" and "The Bible says before you were born, God knew you." The spelling words are the same as in any school; it's the context in which learning takes place that is radically different.

This different context for learning permeates the classroom. In a Georgia school, pupils using Alpha Omega workbooks called "LifePacs" read this introduction to a unit on atoms and molecules:

> Just as we believe in God even though we do not see Him, we will study something even though we do not see it. The existence of atoms is accepted, even though they cannot be seen. Principles in the spiritual realm and in the natural realm often work the same way. As you study atoms and molecules and how they link together, notice that science only goes so far

in explaining things. As Christians we know that the ultimate force that holds things together and maintains natural order is God.

This is absolute Truth in principle. Now for an example of absolute Truth in practice.

Shakespeare's *Macbeth* was the focal point in a twelfth-grade English class at Calvary Baptist Academy in Normal, Illinois. The students had finished reading it, and now the teacher was telling them what it meant. She told the twenty-one students that *Macbeth* is an anatomy of rebellion. "God always rewards wrong with punishment, but sometimes it takes awhile," the teacher said. "So we have to look at the long span of history sometimes to see it." She said Shakespeare's plays, like most of the classics, reward good and punish evil in the end. "The classics are almost all that way. Modern novels aren't. They don't show the rewards of good and the punishment of evil by the end of the novel." The teacher drew a comparison to life itself. "Sometimes it looks like people get away with their sins and that good people aren't rewarded, but we're unable to see the long span of history."

That is absolute Truth in practice. Now for an example of absolute Truth in persuasion.

At the Paw Creek Christian Academy in Charlotte, North Carolina, the world history class was studying Martin Luther, John Calvin and others involved in the revolt and division from the Roman Catholic Church. The teacher taught that Catholicism was in error, that Luther was a hero and that Calvin's views of predestination were misguided. The teacher particularly wanted to persuade students against predestination. "We don't believe in predestination," the teacher told his class. "Now I know this will be hard to imagine, but imagine that I'm God." There were mock oohs and aahs in the class. The teacher, in his first year in the classroom, grinned. "Billy, I've decided beforehand that you are going to hell. No matter what you do or how hard you try, you are going to hell. But I've decided that Angela is going to heaven. You see how silly predestination is."

Christian school educators want doctrinal instruction to accompany history lessons. They want teachers to discuss the eternal punishment of evil when tackling Shakespeare. They want books to tell that science is fallible. Their biggest fear, in fact, is that Christian schools will become so academics oriented that they will lose their spiritual distinctiveness through the years. The Association of Christian Schools International has warned its member schools of the tendency to get "so caught up in providing a superior academic program" that spiritual decline occurs. A newsletter to member schools said:

History is strewn with the bleached bones of educational institutions which are now strong academic entities, but today their original commitment to the centrality of Christ and the authority of the Scriptures have long been forgotten. America's first colleges—Harvard, Yale, Dartmouth—were at one time bastions of evangelistic fervor. While these institutions are now respected academic universities, they have drifted far from their original spiritual foundations.[1]

To prevent a drift from their spiritual foundations, Christian schools sometimes emphasize evangelism ahead of academics. "Last year in our second grade class," said David Linkswiler, principal of Cloverdale Christian Academy in Little Rock, "the teacher was giving a Bible study and she asked if someone wanted to give their lives to the Lord. Three raised their hands. Well, it was time for math. But she threw out her lesson plans. She read the scriptures telling about salvation and made it a class affair. The three were saved, and the parents were very happy."

With math lessons occasionally being postponed for salvation lessons, it's natural for people to wonder about the academic quality of these Christian schools.

Some Christian schools are educationally strong; others are, in the words of a prominent Christian school leader, "a fright." A large fundamentalist school in South Carolina offers a large menu of foreign languages while a small fundamentalist school in Oklahoma offers none. For every Delaware County Christian School in Pennsylvania, with its impressive library and computer science room, there are schools such as the one in rural Alabama with a library consisting of decades of old National Geographics and not much else. Of course, the Pennsylvania school has been in operation more than 30 years. "We view these new fundamentalist schools as our sister schools and we are supportive of them," said the school's development director, Steve Dill. "We'd like to see these schools grow and mature. After all, if you had visited us twenty years ago, you wouldn't have seen a library like we have today. It takes time to develop."

A "product" comparison with the public schools is difficult to make. Christian school administrators usually were eager to reach into their files and show me the results of standardized tests that compared their students to national norms. Various quantitative measurements routinely show Christian school pupils a grade level or two above the national norm. Ron-

---

[1]Paul Kienel, "Evangelism in Christian Schools," *Christian School Comment* (published by the Association of Christian Schools International, January 1986).

ald E. Johnson, vice president of Accelerated Christian Education, cited a CTB McGraw-Hill study of 5,000 first-year students in a sampling of 200 schools using the A.C.E. curriculum. The results: In one year, students who came to A.C.E. schools from public schools showed a one-and-seventenths-year achievement on the California Achievement Test.[2]

The scant amount of available evidence from standardized tests suggests that even unaccredited schools are educationally sound. The thendirector of the Law and Education Center of the Education Commission of the States noted that test scores introduced in lawsuits suggest that children's performances actually improved after their enrollment in unaccredited schools.[3]

Is it that teachers in Christian schools are better, or the curriculum stronger? Not necessarily. Christian schools certainly offer a climate that is conducive to rote learning. But the reason for these favorable test comparisons is more basic. The public school is the melting pot and the Christian school is the hothouse. The public school must seek to teach all who come. The Christian school can be selective. To draw a proper conclusion, then, you'd need to compare the test scores of Christian school pupils with those public school pupils from similar backgrounds.

Another method of comparing educational systems is to look at how the students do in college. No longitudinal data exist, but a Bob Jones University report stamped ''CONFIDENTIAL'' and sent to Christian school principals provides a curious fact. The report, shared by a Christian school principal on the condition he remain anonymous, said graduates of public schools had higher grade-point averages at the university than graduates of Christian schools. In seeking to justify this incongruity, the report speculated that perhaps the university was attracting only the top students from public schools while too many Christian schools were encouraging marginal students to go to college.

There's another possibility. Higher education, and life itself, is based more on free thought than rote memorization. Christian schools have a ten-

---

[2]Specifics of the CTB McGraw-Hill study are given in ''Facts about Accelerated Christian Education'' (an A.C.E. publication, Lewisville TX, 1979) 12. The study showed that the smallest first-year gains among students who came from public schools to A.C.E. schools were in reading vocabulary and language spelling, and the largest gains were in arithmetic fundamentals and reading comprehension.

[3]Patricia Lines, ''State Regulation of Private Education,'' *Phi Delta Kappan* (October 1982): 120. See State v. Shaver, 294 N.W. 2d 883 (N.D., 1980); and In re Rice, 204 Neb. 732, 285 N.W. 2d 223 (1979).

dency to emphasize rote learning and to downplay the importance of free thought. They often are more interested in teaching students answers than in teaching them to ask questions. Intellectual pursuit frequently takes a backseat to intellectual transfer.

The late Christian thinker Francis Schaeffer believed this to be the one great shortcoming of the Christian school movement. I was present at Schaeffer's last public forum before his death from cancer. He talked about how Christian schools needed to work harder at teaching children how to think, to debate, and to analyze. "Christian education should be a broad presentation of ideas, then pointing out which ideas are in agreement and which are in conflict with scripture," he said.

After spending eighteen months observing a strict fundamentalist school in Illinois, education professor Alan Peshkin concluded that it was a good school in conventional terms if the criteria were standardized test scores, the assigning of homework, an orderly school climate conducive to learning, expectations of high student achievement, and other normative educational standards.

Peshkin did note continual efforts by the school to preach the faith and to inculcate respect for authority, but he dismissed the "brainwashing" scenario sometimes painted by critics. "Indoctrination is not uncommon in public schools, notwithstanding the absence there of an articulated, accepted doctrinal basis to the indoctrinational stance of their teachers," Peshkin wrote. "The critical fact is not that one school never indoctrinates and the other one always does, but, rather, that most public schools have built-in diversity in the heterogeneity of their students and teachers."[4]

Peshkin's study of a single fundamentalist school found an amazing homogeneity among its students—at least in belief systems. In 1980, he surveyed 115 students at the fundamentalist school and found that only nine percent said they would go to a public school if they could. The survey showed strong conformity to the norms of the school. Eighty percent agreed they should live separate from the world—be in the world but not adopt the world's standards for living. Three out of four said it was not important to learn to question authority. Two out of three believed they should be close friends *only* with born-again Christians. Nine out of ten said that if they marry, they will marry a born-again Christian. And eighty-seven percent agreed there is only one true religion. Despite this homogeneity in be-

[4]Alan Peshkin, *God's Choice: The Total World of a Fundamentalist Christian School* (Chicago: University of Chicago Press, 1986) 284-85.

liefs, Peshkin concluded after eighteen months in the school that the students, as a group, "seem never to be mindless youth, frozen into routines, beliefs and behavior patterns that control them as though they were machines." He said the children were "recognizably spirited, fun loving, enthusiastic, warm, and friendly." He added:

> I was relieved to find that Bethany's children, even its most "spiritual" ones, are very ordinary Americans in many respects, far from the image of the automoton that critics of Christian schools present. I was further relieved to see that the desired inculcation of doctrine and obedience seldom attained a level of perfection sufficient to preclude personal, individualistic, independent judgment.[5]

Peshkin also drew a representative sample of 104 students from the same grades at the public school in the same community. He found significant differences in student attitudes about the importance of money and about cheating. More than forty percent of the fundamentalist school pupils said having "lots of money" is unimportant, compared with six percent of the public school pupils. If they saw someone cheat, seventy-three percent of the fundamentalist students said they would urge the cheater to report himself and sixty-three percent said they would turn in the cheater themselves if he didn't do so. Only twenty-two percent of the public school students said they would even urge the cheater to report himself.

The survey also reported a profound difference in levels of certainty. When given the statement "The way things are nowadays, I find it difficult to know just what to believe," seventy-six percent of the fundamentalist school students disagreed while seventy-nine percent of the public school students agreed. A machiavellian scale given to both groups of students found that fundamentalist school pupils were significantly less alienated and significantly more certain than public school students in the same community.

Christian school students find security in the absoluteness of their religion. But, as Peshkin noted, this certainty may come at the expense of other attributes. He wrote:

> I do not see how Bethany's ideal of Christian schooling from kindergarten through college can avoid promoting intransigence, since students neither learn the habit of compromise nor grasp its necessity in a diverse, complex society. Furthermore, I do not see students learning that dissent

---

[5]Ibid., 297.

and compromise are critical attributes of healthy democracies, rather than unwelcome guests in the house of orthodoxy.[6]

Because students in these schools are taught absolutes in living, compromise, in their eyes, is falling short of what God intends.

Christian schooling is serious business. The virtues of hard work and success are extolled daily since the motive for learning is so serious—the "good grammar is a good testimony" concept. From Day One, students in these schools are taught to excel. They are taught, in fact, that excelling is a way of giving glory to God. Moments of public success—being praised by a teacher in front of the class or your peers finding out you made an A on the exam—are not embarrassing moments for Christian school pupils. Success is not something to get embarrassed about.

But with success must come the possibility of failure. Without the potential for failure, success wouldn't mean much. In the classroom, teachers praise the virtues of competition and the free-enterprise system for this reason. They teach that failure must be permitted to reward success.

Students who go to these schools are drilled to have a strong drive to succeed. They want to have that good testimony. Certainly there is a degree of spiritual playacting involved at times. But students in these schools are not playacting their spirituality all of the time. They really believe.

Yet students are students, no matter what system they are in, and they have safety valves when the pace gets tiresome. For instance, when an English teacher left her room momentarily at Jerry Falwell's junior high academy, a handful of students immediately started tearing parts of blank pages from their spiral notebooks, giving the pieces a quick saliva washing, and then chunking the spitballs at one another. One boy stood guard at the door and brought the impromptu spitball fight to a halt by announcing that the teacher was coming back down the hall. The class had enjoyed the interlude and, if the teacher noticed the spitballs on the floor, she said nothing.

Like adolescents in any school, or for that matter adults at work, those students who attend Christian academies like to break from the mold now and then. They tell jokes—clean ones, usually—and pass notes and play practical jokes. They also can be witty. The topic in an eighth-grade history class in Memphis one day was the causes of World War I. The teacher explained how the assassination of Archduke Ferdinand was the spark that ignited the war, although war eventually would have occurred anyway. The

---

[6]Ibid., 296.

teacher asked a student what happened to the archduke's assassin. The student answered, with a touch of sarcasm toward the judicial system: "He pleaded innocent by reason of insanity and is free on bail." The teacher and the students laughed and then got on with the lesson.

There is not a supercharged undercurrent of tension at these schools. Students aren't on the verge of rebellion. They are not trying to create a new regimen. They almost uniformly accept the school's norms. A boy may complain about having to get a haircut or a girl may complain about having to wear a dress when the temperature outdoors is below freezing, but these are incidentals. When it comes to the spiritual atmosphere, the values taught and the academics emphasized, the schools and the students are in almost total agreement.

15

THE FUTURE
OF
CHRISTIAN SCHOOLS

Fred McNiel walked down the hall-
way of the Christian school he heads in Waco, Texas. While greeting students on their way to class, he turned to me and casually remarked: "You
know, I want my school to be like the one I went to twenty-five years ago."

The comment may not seem particularly illuminating. But his remark
goes a long way toward explaining the phenomenal growth of Christian
schools. Those in the forefront of the Christian school movement idealize
the public schools of twenty-five years ago for stressing the three R's. They
have an image of teachers as authority figures, paddling children who dared
to disobey. They remember textbooks portraying the traditional family.

They recall a time when parents were active and involved, with each school serving its own homogeneous community. They remember the school day beginning with a Bible verse and prayer. They are anxious to recreate these images in their own schools.

Many of today's Christian school educators are wanting to mirror the public schools as they remember them. Others have gone even further back in time, to the era of the one-room schoolhouse and to workbooks that resemble the moralizing McGuffey Readers of a century ago.

The Christian school movement voices a nostalgia for the security of the past. It yearns for a return to "old-time religion" and "old-fashioned virtues." It looks back wistfully to what it perceives as a golden era, a simpler time.

We are witnessing in the Christian school movement a vehement rejection of contemporary America. The intent now is separation, not the melting-pot pluralism of years gone by. That's because the meaning of pluralism has undergone a radical redefinition in America in the past two decades.

In this nation's early years, pluralism meant the merging of various nationalities, religions, languages, and concepts into one—"the American way." Those who did not acculturate were left out. Our public schools were designed to fulfill this historic acculturation process. We standardized the education process to "Americanize" the nation. Since all of society was then dominated by Protestant values and concepts, this acculturation process was firmly rooted in cultural Protestantism. Jews and Catholics were tolerated as essential to the country's notion of religious freedom. In this form of religious pluralism, differences were discussed within the context of the cultural Protestantism that reigned.

Today, pluralism means the right to be "American" without acculturation. Frankly, no one expected cultural Protestantism ever to be challenged as the symbolic model of America. But the redefinition of pluralism in this country after World War II changed all of this. The prevailing hegemony became unglued and, quite suddenly, there was no longer one dominant set of cultural values. Church attendance dropped precipitously. In 1960, the American people said they no longer had to have a Protestant as president. Then the Supreme Court, with its prayer and Bible-reading rulings, refused to let the public schools continue two of the outward symbols of cultural Protestantism. Quite suddenly, cultural Protestantism no longer indisputably served as this nation's defining authority.

In turn, the educational establishment responded by formulating value-free education, or what goes by the name of secularism. Instead of espousing particular values, the public schools began to espouse the value of the *search* for values. Maybe that was all they could legitimately do. But this transformation to a secular educational system led to rebellion by those still adhering to the values of cultural Protestantism.

Many in the Christian community no longer accept the ideal of the public school as melting pot, because the melting pot no longer is based on the values of cultural Protestantism. Rather than acculturate into a society they see as having gone bad, the intent instead has become the building of an alternative Christian community.

The Christian school is one of the building blocks of a society within a society—a Christian community within the larger secular one. Besides going to church on Sunday, Christians now can listen to Christian radio stations when they wake up and watch Christian TV when they go to bed. They can read Christian books for inspiration. They can plan their recreation around Christian family life centers at their churches. They can do business only with born-again businessmen through the "Christian Yellow Pages." And for the children, there are Christian schools.

This society-within-a-society concept runs perpendicular to the very concept that now serves as its protector. The Christian school owes much to the concept of pluralism in our secularized society, but pluralism is seldom extolled in its classrooms.

"Espousing pluralism is not functional to the cause of their monolithic Truth," wrote education professor Alan Peshkin after spending eighteen months inside a fundamentalist school in Illinois. "Rather than tussle with the dilemmas produced by the acceptance of both pluralism and absolute, universal truth, they leave the principle of pluralism as an abstraction, one that is literally overwhelmed by their Truth and its ramifications."[1]

This leads to a paradox. The existence of Christian schools attests to the well-being of our pluralistic society. However, because their absolutist views of Truth prevent their support of pluralism, they actually seek to undermine the principle that guarantees their existence. "The existence of fundamentalist Christian schools creates a paradox of pluralism in the United States," Peshkin concludes. "Paradoxes of pluralism testify to our ideological health."[2]

---

[1]Alan Peshkin, *God's Choice: The Total World of a Fundamentalist Christian School* (Chicago: University of Chicago Press, 1986) 293.

[2]Ibid., 298.

In other words, Christian schools represent educational pluralism at its fullest. Yet these very schools that represent pluralism at its fullest are, ironically, antipluralistic. They seek not to promote pluralism but, instead, to preach separatism.

The tension that exists between our desire for cultural pluralism and our desire to establish a common cultural base leads to another paradox, namely, educational alternatives can be viewed as a threat to the democratic way. The concept of educational pluralism means alternate schools have the right to exist. Yet many in this country view education as the prerogative of the state, and thus view the public school as the only real democratic instrument for educating children.

"There are so many people who really believe the democratic system is based on the public schools," said Dr. Philip Elve, formerly with Christian Schools International in Grand Rapids, Michigan. "In the same breath, they will talk about public education and the American way. They think they are one and the same. They don't recognize that democratic principles are based on diversity. They seem to forget that's the basis of a democracy. Instead, they want a monolithic, monopolistic type of education which is only kindred to totalitarian states. And in some strange way of thinking, they have said that totalitarian way of doing a school system is the American way, the democratic way. You'd think that a person who really believes in a democracy and in individual freedom of choice would say we ought to have a great variety of educational choices. But in some way of twisted thinking, they come to the opposite conclusion and they view the nonpublic school as threatening to the democratic way."

The perceived threat is nowhere more evident than in the battle over tuition tax credits and voucher systems. Greater acceptance of private education raises the likelihood of a further exodus from the public schools if money becomes less of an object to parents. So the financial battle carries high stakes. Albert Shanker, president of the American Federation of Teachers, doesn't mince words: "At the end of the decade, most Americans might be sending their children to private schools and getting government subsidies to do it. We plan to fight like hell against it."[3]

The Christian school movement is philosophically aligned to conservative, Republican politics. With a president in office who supports tuition tax credits for private schools, public school advocates are understandably

---

[3]Gene Maeroff, "Private Schools Look to Bright Future," *The New York Times,* 4 January 1981, 1.

worried. Their once-impregnable base of support is gradually eroding as private schooling becomes more popular and as the New Right becomes more politically powerful. Legislation to allow taxpayers to deduct portions of their children's school tuition has died in previous sessions of the Congress, but support grows year by year.

On the state level, the foot inside the tax-deduction door has been achieved in Minnesota. In 1983, the U.S. Supreme Court in a five-to-four vote upheld a Minnesota law that allows parents to claim state tax deducations for their children's school expenses.[4] Supporters of the law successfully argued that the law is neutral because parents of public school also may take deductions. Opponents argued, without success, that the cost of attending public schools is so low that the law was merely a thinly disguised effort to help those who send their children to private schools. Buoyed by the Court ruling, at least eight other states are considering tuition tax deduction or tax credit plans.[5]

A voucher system also is generating interest. Some states are considering legislation to allow low-income families to use the state's average per pupil expenditure as a downpayment toward attending any public or private school in that state.

A Christian school principal in Texas who favors the voucher concept doesn't blame public school lobbies and teacher unions for fighting the proposals. "The public schools already have lost the rich," he said. "Now they're scared of losing the poor."

Surprisingly, no consensus exists in the Christian school community on the tuition tax credit and voucher concepts. While either one would help open the Christian schoolhouse doors to more parents, fundamentalists fear the eventual attachment of government strings.

"Our movement is almost exclusively against any kind of government funding, against any kind of government regulation and very skeptical of the tuition tax credit scheme because of what we feel would be almost sure strings attached," said Dr. Gerald B. Carlson of the American Association of Christian Schools.

The push for tuition tax credits has come primarily from the Catholic school lobby. But to succeed in Congress, the Catholics need the fundamentalists. "They need our support because of our ties to conservative politicians," Carlson said. To gain that support, recent proposals in Con-

---

[4]Mueller v. Allen, 463 U.S. 388 (1983).

[5]"When Church and State Collide," *U.S. News & World Report* (5 March 1984): 42-43.

gress have specified that nothing in the tax legislation should be construed to cause government intervention in private education.

Public school supporters paint a bleak scenario for public education if tax benefits are provided to parents who send their children to private schools. Some plainly predict that America's public schools would be reserved for the poor and the handicapped while the rest of the nation's children attend private schools. They fear that, in this nation's vast mosaic of 82,000 public schools and another 25,000 or so private and religious schools, the public schools could eventually become the educational scrap heap for the poorest and least motivated children in the nation's underclass.

Some in the Christian school movement agree with that bleak assessment. Others believe the public schools simply have been in a down cycle for a decade and already are improving with an infusion of new money and commitment. Still others believe the public schools will regain support only when competition from private education forces them to improve their quality.

Meanwhile, enrollment in Christian schools shows no signs of reversing direction.

"I see the Christian school movement booming through the '80s and '90s. It will be very strong," principal Rick Carter said while watching his students play outside Bible Baptist Christian School in Gulfport, Mississippi. "Until now, Americans didn't have an alternative. When there's no competition, you can be as sorry as can be and people still have to go to you. A lot of the future depends on the public schools."

Predicts Michael Healan, principal of Hartford Christian Academy in Connecticut: "The success of the Christian schools is going to be a real source of embarrassment for the public schools. In the areas of discipline and academic excellence, we'll see some improvement in the public schools. But they'll never be back where they were in the '50s. They've moved too far away."

At the all-black Christian school in Baton Rouge, academic dean Mrs. Glenda Colbert declared: "I don't think the public schools will make it. God has come out of the public schools. They'll just eventually go by the wayside. We'll turn again to the churches to educate the children."

Christian political activist Tim LaHaye adds: "Never in my lifetime has public education been so unpopular with the rank and file. I think the Christian school movement and the home school movement will mushroom in the future."

If the Christian school movement is a sign of cultural separation, then the home school movement is even more so. Christian parents by the thousands are opting not to send their children to *any* school but, instead, to teach them at home. The A.C.E. and the A Beka Book curricula are particularly popular among Christians who have chosen to teach their children around the kitchen table. Since the A.C.E. program does not require teacher preparation, many parents find it ideal.

A few Christian schools accommodate partial home instruction. For instance, the Living Word Christian School in St. Charles, Missouri, offers a four-day-a-week program for parents who want to keep their children home one day a week for personal instruction. This is not a common practice, though.

"Christian schools should put an umbrella over these home schools and help them by providing instruction, curriculum, and testing," LaHaye said. "They should build a relationship so that, when it's time to go to a classroom, they'll be ready." LaHaye believes a structured school setting is not vital until the fourth or fifth grades. "Educators brainwashed parents into the idea that children should be taken away from their parents and sent to a public school when they are five years old. That's way too early." LaHaye's daughter is teaching her two young children at home, using Christian literature. "The home school resolves this whole twentieth-century phenomenon of separating parents and their children for long periods of time."

I visited a home school in the St. Louis area where three college-educated mothers alternate as teachers for their young children. A basement in one of the homes serves as the school. Children learn the alphabet by memorizing a Bible verse beginning with each letter. The parents say they eventually will place their children in a Christian school, but for now they want to have control over their children's learning. Socialization for the children comes from having more than one family participate in a home school.

Nationwide, the number of children attending home schools has grown from an estimated 10,000 in the mid-1970s to 50,000 in the mid-1980s.[6] Many of these home schools are operating in defiance of state compulsory

---

[6]Patricia Lines, "The New Private Schools and Their Historic Purpose," *Phi Delta Kappan* (January 1986): 377. Books that give practical advice on home schooling are Raymond and Dorothy Moore's *Home-Grown Kids* (Waco TX: Word Books, 1981); *Home-Spun Schools* (Waco TX: Word Books, 1982); and *Home-Style Teaching* (Waco TX: Word Books, 1984).

education laws. States are struggling with the issue. Some have made home schools legitimate; others say that would make school attendance laws unenforceable. "We're seeing a lot of home schools in North Carolina," an official in the state attorney general's office told me. "I think public pressure will keep Christian schools up to snuff, but home schools don't have that check and balance. How will we know if a child is being educated or not?"

Considering that all education in this nation once came from either the home or the church, it is ironic that we have developed such a suspicion toward private forms of education.

Catholic schools today are accepted as valid alternative schools. These new Protestant schools have yet to reach that level of public acceptance. The timing of their genesis has much to do with it. Many people view all of these schools as racist. The movement also is so separatist in nature that few outsiders understand it. No new movement is broad-based; it appeals first to its own kind. The test is how broad it will become. Catholic schools have been around for more than a century now. It will take time for Protestant schools to become a similarly accepted part of the educational mosaic.

The former director of the Law and Education Center for the Education Commission of the States draws a comparison between the Catholic and Protestant school movements. Patricia Lines writes:

> The availability of private education works to accommodate minorities. At two points, in particular, private schools have been a refuge for those who dissent from the value system explicitly or implicitly adopted by the public schools. When public school values were Protestant, a vigorous Roman Catholic school system emerged. Now that public school values are secular, a strong Protestant private school movement has emerged.[7]

In fact, if present trends continue, Catholic schools no longer will enroll the majority of the private school population. From the middle of the nineteenth century until the mid-1960s, well over ninety percent of the children in private schools were in Catholic schools. But while Catholic school enrollment has sharply dropped since the mid-1960s, Christian school enrollment has sharply increased. Lines said this dramatic shift within the private school population coincides with the change in the re-

---

[7]Lines, "The New Private Schools," 373-74.

ligious orientation of the public schools—the shift from cultural Protestantism to secularism. Lines concluded that many Catholics now regard public schools as safe for their children, while an increasing number of Protestants do not.[8]

Since the Protestant orientation of the public schools has disappeared, private schooling has become a viable option for Protestant dissent and separation.

Author Jeremy Rifkin calls the Christian school movement "a revolution of such magnitude that even its few close observers are reluctant to make more than a few tentative predictions as to the effect it will have on American society over the next half century."[9] He adds:

> No one really knows if or when the Christian school movement will begin to show signs of slowing down. In the meantime, its phenomenal growth is already serving as a testimonial to both the seriousness of the Christian revival taking place and the determination of evangelicals to forge an alternative Christian community within the country.[10]

New Christian schools are sprouting all across the nation. "The Christian school movement is a fraction of what it probably will become," ACSI's Paul Kienel said. "I am doubtful the public schools will do anything to regain the confidence of the evangelical Protestant community. As the wall of alienation continues between the evangelical Protestant community and the public schools, those who are currently loyal to the public schools will fall away."

Kienel said the Christian school movement still has the sympathy of only twenty percent of the evangelical Protestant community. The fourteen-million-member Southern Baptist Convention—the largest religious body in the United States outside the Roman Catholic Church—is on record as supporting the public schools.

"I don't think we have won our own crowd over yet," Kienel said. "There is a latent loyalty in the evangelical Protestant community to the public school that is hard to shake. But as the public school image becomes more and more bizarre, they're going to lose that eighty percent still clinging to them."

---

[8]Ibid., 374.

[9]Jeremy Rifkin, *The Emerging Order: God in the Age of Scarcity* (New York: Ballantine Books, 1979) 115.

[10]Ibid., 117.

He sees signs of that already happening. Although the Southern Baptist Convention is encouraging its people to stick with the public schools, each church is autonomous and the more conservative churches are starting Christian schools. Some black churches in Watts, Kansas City, Detroit, and even in rural areas have started Christian schools. The Christian school movement also cuts across doctrinal lines, from the fundamentalists to the charismatics to the mainline Protestants.

"You have to realize things can compound very quickly," Kienel said. "Five or six years ago, very few of our schools occupied public school facilities. Now many of them do." Down the street from Kienel's office, Whittier Christian High was embarking on its third public school takeover. Calumet Baptist School in Gary, Indiana, is in an abandoned public school. Hartford Christian Academy in Connecticut meets in a public school building that was closed because of declining enrollment. Delaware County Christian School in Pennsylvania decided to pay $330,000 to purchase a vacant public school building two miles away to handle the Christian school's overflow of students.

We are back again to the public schools. Can they ever regain the confidence of fundamentalist Christians? It is doubtful at this point. The Christian school movement has gone too far down the separatist path to turn back now. These parents are concerned about the direction of society, yes; but their overriding concern is for the value system imparted to their children. For this reason, their withdrawal from the public schools will only accelerate.

So Christian educators forge ahead in their mission to educate the young through biblical principles in hopes of producing a Christian America again. "I want to produce young people who can stand up to their peers and say, 'No, that's not right' without being obnoxious," said Dr. Walter Barge Sr., founder of Grace Heritage School in Research Triangle Park, North Carolina. "If we can make Christian schools strong enough academically but not too narrow, it may very well produce the leaven to reproduce Christian values in our society."

Reaching into a file cabinet in his office, administrator Glen Schultz of Lynchburg Christian Academy in Virginia produced this statement by futurist Alvin Toffler:

All education springs from some image of the future. If the image of the future held by a society is grossly inaccurate, its education system will betray its youth.[11]

---

[11]Alvin Toffler, ed., *Learning for Tomorrow: The Role of the Future in Education* (New

Schultz believes this is America's situation today. He believes the public schools have an inaccurate image of the future and thus are unconsciously betraying the youth. "In reality," he says, "our image of the future is different from theirs."

Do Christian schools have a more accurate image of the future? That is a decision each of us must make individually as parents and as citizens.

York: Random House, 1974) 3.

INDEX